THE EASTERN CARPET IN THE WESTERN WORLD

FROM THE 15TH TO THE 17TH CENTURY

Selected and arranged by Donald King
and David Sylvester

Hayward Gallery, London
20 May – 10 July 1983

Arts Council
OF GREAT BRITAIN

Presented by the Arts Council as part of
The Oriental Carpet in London 1983 on the occasion of
The Fourth International Conference on Oriental Carpets,
Barbican Centre, London, 9–12 June 1983

Exhibition organized by Susan Ferleger Brades,
assisted by Jocelyn Poulton

Exhibition design consultant: Neave Brown

Catalogue designed by Trevor Vincent
Map drawn by Brian and Constance Dear
Printed in England by Jolly & Barber Limited, Rugby

ISBN 0 7287 0362 9

A list of Arts Council publications, including
all exhibition catalogues in print,
can be obtained from the Publications Officer,
Arts Council of Great Britain,
105 Piccadilly, London W IV OAU

COVER
The Somerset House Conference, 1604 (detail)
Painting by an unknown artist, 1604
Reproduced by permission of the Trustees of the
National Portrait Gallery, London, no. 665 (fig. 1)

FRONT ENDPAPER
Vittore Carpaccio, *St. Ursula Cycle* (detail), *c.* 1495
Accademia, Venice

BACK ENDPAPER
School or follower of Moretto
Fresco (detail), before 1543
Martinengo – Salvadego Palace, Brescia

PAGE 105
Giovanni Mansueti (1485–1526)
Procession from Santa Croce to San Lio (detail)
(photo courtesy Cameraphoto, Venice)

Contents

Lenders

The Walters Art Gallery, Baltimore: 54
Staatliche Museen Preussischer Kulturbesitz, Museum für Islamische Kunst, Berlin: 16, 42, 77, 78
Museum of Fine Arts, Boston: 7, 23, 57
Museum and Art Gallery, Bristol: 84
Museum of Applied Arts (Iparmüvészeti Muzeum), Budapest: 11, 14, 15, 34, 47, 48
Soprintendenza per i Beni Artistici e Storici, Florence: 21, 56
The National Trust, Hardwick Hall: 36
Calouste Gulbenkian Museum, Lisbon: 58
Victoria and Albert Museum, London: 9, 13, 17, 38, 49, 52, 75, 82
Musée Historique des Tissus, Lyon: 61
Bayerisches Nationalmuseum, Munich: 26
Bayerische Verwaltung der Staatlichen Schlösser, Gärten und Seen, Residenzmuseum, Munich: 73
The Brooklyn Museum, New York: 63
The Metropolitan Museum of Art, New York: 62, 67, 69
Mobilier National, Paris: 60, 68
Musée des Arts Décoratifs, Paris: 46, 50
Musée du Louvre, Paris: 66, 72
Philadelphia Museum of Art: 28
The Saint Louis Art Museum: 10, 31, 40
Statens Historiska Museum, Stockholm: 2
Österreichisches Museum für angewandte Kunst, Vienna: 22, 30, 74
The Corcoran Gallery of Art, Washington, D.C.: 80
The Textile Museum, Washington, D.C.: 4, 5, 18, 25, 27, 29, 43, 59, 86

Bernheimer Collection, Munich: 12
His Grace The Duke of Buccleuch & Queensberry, K.T.: 32, 33, 37, 70
John Hewett: 81
Harold Mark Keshishian: 39
The Keir Collection: 6, 83
The Royal Collections, Stockholm: 65
Thyssen-Bornemisza Collection, Lugano, Switzerland: 41, 64, 71, 79, 85
Wher Collection, Switzerland: 8, 35, 44, 45, 53
Private Collections: 24, 76

Foreword

This exhibition is one of several planned to coincide with The Fourth International Conference on Oriental Carpets taking place in London this June.

It is the first major carpet exhibition held in London since 1972, though important carpets were shown in the exhibition of works from the Burrell Collection at the Hayward in 1975, in an exhibition of kilim rugs at the Whitechapel Art Gallery in 1977, and most notably in the World of Islam Festival in 1976. The Festival also included one exhibition exclusively of carpets, organized by Dr May Beattie, which was shown in Sheffield and Birmingham.

The *Islamic Carpets* exhibition which was arranged by the Arts Council at the Hayward in 1972 and which marked, perhaps even created, a widening interest in carpets as great works of art, was devoted to carpets from a single outstanding collection. The present exhibition is organized around a theme, the importation of eastern carpets into Europe at the time of the Renaissance, and gathers its examples from collections throughout the world.

Donald King, former Keeper of Textiles at the Victoria and Albert Museum, and David Sylvester, who organized the 1972 exhibition, have jointly devised, selected and arranged *The Eastern Carpet in the Western World*. To try and disentangle their respective roles, it might be said that the initiative in selection has lain with Donald King and the initiative in presentation with David Sylvester. We are deeply indebted to them both, as we are to Michael Franses, who has been responsible for the lighting and has also given invaluable advice on other aspects of the display and on the selection.

The Textile Conservation Centre at Hampton Court has prepared many of the carpets for display. We are very grateful for the support of Karen Finch, Principal of the Centre, and of Caroline Clark, Head of the Tapestry Department, as well as to the Centre's staff and students for the help they have given us.

It is paintings – as our cover picture suggests – that are the primary source of knowledge on the arrival of oriental carpets in Europe, and this summer's exhibitions include one at the National Gallery which brings together paintings from their collection in which eastern carpets are depicted. Its organizer, John Mills, has contributed to our exhibition by scripting an audio-visual programme which provides an essential complement to the display of the carpets and ranges far and wide in the world's picture collections. We are grateful to him and also to Darryl Johnson of the Triangle Audio Visual Partnership for producing the programme.

Our catalogue is intended to enlarge on the theme of the exhibition as well as to provide information on the origin and history of the carpets included in it. We should like to thank all the contributors, particularly Donald King, who wrote the catalogue under very considerable pressure of time.

Our greatest debt is to the lenders, both public and private, who are listed on the facing page. For reasons beyond our control, and that of the selectors, we were unable to make our loan requests until later than is normal for an international exhibition of this complexity. However, museums and private owners responded promptly and with great generosity. We hope that the exhibition will be as memorable as the last Hayward Gallery carpets exhibition.

Joanna Drew *Director of Art*

The Islamic World and the West
15th–17th century

1 *The Somerset House Conference, 1604*
  Painting by an unknown artist, 1604
  Reproduced by permission of the Trustees of the National Portrait Gallery,
  London, no. 665 (detail on the cover)

The Eastern Carpet in the Western World from the 15th to the 20th century

David Sylvester

Our cover picture of an eastern carpet in the western world does not in fact portray the trustees of a great museum in the course of considering its purchase. On the contrary, the carpet is depicted in an altogether healthy situation. This artefact imported from an alien culture is shown to be used, cherished, given a central place at great occasions. The occasion is the peace conference between England and Spain in 1604, and the cherishing is indicated by the fact (demonstrated in John Mills's essay) that the carpet was an old one. While cherished, it is not neurotically conserved but allowed to play a part in life. Spread out as a no-man's land between the opposing teams of great sly men of state, its bright geometry presents them with a paradigm of forthright statement, ingenious design, perfect organization and radiant harmony.

The picture also seems to demonstrate that western painters accorded a welcome of their own to these imports. There may have been no option for the composition but to put the carpet in the centre of the stage, but that carpet is painted with a loving involvement that is a true exercise of art in celebration of another art.

The crucial fact not evident in the picture is that the countries represented at the table, beyond making such imports a part of their lives, were active in manufacturing carpets which imitated and adapted them – in particular, the styles of 15th and 16th century Turkish carpets such as this one. Here, even such notable English achievements as the carpet dated 1603 in the Victoria and Albert Museum (fig. 27 in Donald King's text) are over-shadowed by the remarkable tradition created in Spain – reaching its peak in the 15th century but continuing into the 17th – of adapting Turkish prototypes into something at once distinctly European and perhaps of even higher artistic quality. Of all the instances in the world's arts and crafts of the absorption and transformation of a foreign language, it would be difficult to think of any that was more successful. Nothing could testify better to the health of the relationship of the western world to the eastern carpet then.

If the situation now of eastern carpets in our world is a less healthy one, it is not a priori because the better examples are sooner or later withdrawn from life and lodged, away from wear and tear and ultra-violet, in museums. The removal of any valued object to its place of rest in a museum is a fairly inevitable stage in its life-cycle – life-cycle because an object in a museum fertilizes new growth, engenders it, indeed. In practice, however, museum acquisitions of carpets are generally undesirable events – except in terms of conservation – because they tend to ensure that those carpets will never again be seen as they ought to be – on the ground or a table (and unglazed). This is not the fault of specialist curatorial staff. It derives from the fact that most of the world's museums with sizeable holdings of carpets do not have – or do not assign – the space needed to show them properly, even to show more than a few of them at all.

Showing them properly would not stop at displaying them on the ground (and unglazed). They cannot be fully experienced if they can only be walked round: to be unable to stand in the middle of a carpet is to be insulated from its full impact as one would be from that of a cathedral where one was not permitted to move down the nave. The aesthetic of the carpet demands that the spectator needs to be – *or at least to feel* – surrounded by its form and colour (which is why fragments of carpets tend not to work as well on the floor as on the wall). In a public gallery the nearest practical substitute for standing on a carpet is to be able to view it from a higher level. The present exhibition has a few such vantage points (with opera glasses provided). These will, perhaps, more than compensate for its presenting less pieces on the floor than did the 1972 carpets exhibition at the Hayward, which, though less distinguished, occupied the entire gallery, as this one has not been able to do.

If carpet exhibitions happen too rarely and are then too cramped, it is because their public, though increasing, is still a limited one, and it is, of course, for the same reason that museums go on being parsimonious with the space they allocate. The present-day relationship between the western world and the eastern carpet is epitomized in the living-rooms of most people who pride themselves on their awareness of the visual arts. Along with good pictures and sculptures and furniture, south of the skirting-board there'll be rubbish.

The Coming of the Carpet to the West

John Mills

Pile carpets were quite probably known in Greece and Rome in classical times. This was taken for granted by many of the earlier carpet historians of the 19th century who pointed to many references to them in Greek and Latin literature as well as still earlier references in the Old Testament.[1] Many different terms were used for them and there was no certain way of knowing what techniques were employed in their manufacture. Some of the references pointed to an origin in the Near East as did also the apparent representation of a pile carpet in the famous 'stone carpet' in the alabaster threshold from 7th century BC Nineveh, now in the British Museum. That some of these carpets were in truth pile carpets such as we know today became a near certainty with the discovery, in central Asia in 1949, of an almost complete pile carpet[2] which was subsequently dated (by C14 dating of its associated grave goods) to the 3rd to 5th century BC. By a striking coincidence (for there must have existed many different designs) the field design was very similar to that of the 'stone carpet' of Nineveh.

After the fall of Rome the history of the carpet in western Europe is a closed book for the next eight hundred years or so but it is certain that carpets of some kind continued to be made and used within the boundaries of the Byzantine Empire. Coptic rugs of the 5th century, made in a form of looped pile technique, have survived[3] and there are references to the use of 'soft rugs' on the floors of churches in Constantinople[4] which were probably something of this kind.

It may have been indirectly via Egypt that carpets and carpet weaving were reintroduced to western Europe. With the rise and expansion of Islam in the 7th century the Arabs swept across Egypt and North Africa gathering Egyptian and Berber converts to their forces. The polyglot armies of Moors or Saracens, as they were called in Europe, invaded and swiftly conquered the whole of Visigothic Spain in the early 8th century. Later in the century the city of Cordoba was founded and developed into a great centre of art and learning. Production of textiles of different kinds soon became widespread but when rugs were first woven is not known exactly. The earliest mentions[5] are in the 12th century and refer to rugs of Chinchilla, in Murcia, said to be exported to all countries. In 13th century France they were called *tapis Sarrasinois*, many having been seized in wars against the Moors by Louis IX.

The Moors' domination of the whole of Spain did not last long and they had been driven out of the North already in the 9th century to be confined to Andalusia. Their textile products were, however, much in demand by the Christian kingdoms of the North and it was one of these which was responsible for what was doubtless the first sight of woven carpets in England. When Eleanor of Castile came to London to marry the future Edward I in 1255 she brought with her as part of her dowry a number of tapestries and carpets with which she decorated the walls and floors of her lodgings in the Temple in Westminster. Apparently this luxurious display was the butt of much sarcasm and abuse from the citizens of London. Certainly there was no way it could be emulated by them for carpets were not to arrive in any numbers for at least another three hundred years.

We do not know what these early Hispano-Moresque carpets looked like for nothing has survived of them. Many large carpets do however survive from the 15th century when they were still being woven by Moors remaining in cities of re-Christianized Spain – so-called Mudejars. Similar designs to those in these 'armorial star pattern' carpets must have been woven in the preceding century for one is to be seen in a fresco in the Palace of the Popes in Avignon (fig. 2). These frescos show scenes from the life of St. Martial and were carried out for Clement VI by the resident painter Matteo di Giovanetti in 1344–6. A scene of the saint reviving two pagan priests shows a large carpet on the floor. A previous pope, John XXII (reigned 1316–34), is said to have ordered carpets from Spain, so this could have been one of them. His successor Benedict XII was said to be fond of Turkish rugs, particularly one with white swans. Curiously the above fresco also shows a rug with large spotted birds.[6] In the 14th century, during the residence of the papacy at Avignon, there would not have been the least difficulty in obtaining goods from the Mediterranean countries or other areas of Europe. The Italian merchant Francesco Datini of Prato, whose correspondence and documents have survived almost *in toto*, lived in Avignon from 1350 to 1382 and has left us a vivid picture of the mercantile life of the period.[7] He had extensive dealings in Spain but unfortunately no references in his correspondence to carpets have so far been reported.

The Avignon fresco is of very special interest as it is the only representation in a 14th century painting of a carpet of whose country of origin we can be perfectly sure, and it comes at the beginning of the period in which actual visual records – the appearances of carpets in paintings – tell us much about the designs of the weavings in use at a given place and time. Before this we have to be content with simple written records, in inventories, books, letters and

2 Matteo di Giovanetti,
Scenes from the Life of St. Martial (detail), 1344–6,
fresco, showing a Spanish armorial star design carpet.
Palace of the Popes, Avignon.

11

wills, with all their uncertainties as to the meanings of particular terms and their vagueness as to techniques and designs. The paintings in question are, overwhelmingly, those of Italy and it is to the sequence of carpets that these present to us that we will first turn.

Carpets in Italy

Near Eastern carpets must have come to be known in Italy at the latest by the 13th century. The taking of Constantinople after the diversion of the Fourth Crusade in 1204 must have familiarized the crusaders, who included many Venetians, with all the luxurious products of Byzantium and the adjacent territories under Seljuk Turkish control. The Venetians must have sent back some carpets to Venice: they were, after all, able to send back the horses of San Marco, though these of course proved more durable. The 13th century saw the flowering and the decline of the Seljuk administration in Anatolia, and large and splendid carpets were made there during this period as Marco Polo, among others, reported. We can be fairly sure as to what one group of these looked like since the famous group of complete and fragmentary carpets found early this century in the mosque of Ala-ad-din in Konya is rather generally believed to date from the late 13th or early 14th century. Carpets like these may well have been brought to Italy but if they were no fragment, even, has survived nor is there any record of them, either written

3 Florentine School, *Madonna and Child Enthroned*, first half 14th century, showing carpet with splayed eagles. Staatliche Museen Preussischer Kulturbesitz, Gemäldegalerie, Berlin.

4 Miniature of the *Despot Constantine of Bulgaria* in *The Gospels of Tsar Ivan Alexander* (detail), 1355–6 showing Byzantine textile with splayed eagle design. The British Library, London.

or pictorial. There are no representations in paintings of before about 1300 of anything that can plausibly be accepted as a carpet, and nothing thereafter which much resembles the Konya carpets. It has been claimed that Giotto depicted one in his frescos in the upper church of S. Francesco in Assisi but it is not so. The resemblance is fortuitous for the pattern is clearly on tiles which cover the whole floor of the scene shown. Small rugs with geometrical designs do occur in paintings in the 14th century but they are quite few and cannot definitely be attributed to any place of origin. By way of example one could mention an *Annunciation* by Jacopo di Cione in the church of Sto. Spirito in Prato which shows a rug divided up by bands into rectangular compartments containing geometrical motifs, while from the earlier part of the century comes a painting by a Perugian follower of Meo da Siena, in the Museo Nazionale dell 'Umbria in L'Aquila, which shows a small rug with octagonal compartments of which however only the edges appear. These serve merely to indicate that small geometric rugs existed at this time and into the next century.

More interesting than these, and far more abundant in paintings, are carpets showing stylized animals and birds[8] which, despite this common feature, probably do not constitute a homogeneous group. A small sub-group of these shows splayed eagles or rather spidery-looking birds in octagonal, sometimes hexagonal, compartments. Examples are to be seen in paintings by Giotto or his school, the *Stefaneschi Polyptych* in the Vatican and two predella panels of the *Stigmatization of St. Francis* in the Louvre. One also appears in a Florentine School *Madonna and Child Enthroned* (fig. 3). These are all of the first half of the 14th century. The splayed eagle motif also occurs on Byzantine textiles at this time (fig. 4) and it is possible that the carpets (if they are such) are also Byzantine.

A larger sub-group of these early animal carpets in paintings shows, within octagonal compartments, either single standing birds (two examples, the most notable being in the *Marriage of the Virgin* by Niccolò di Buonacorso, the National Gallery, London) or two birds flanking a stylized tree. There are some fourteen examples of the latter design, all of them in paintings of the Sienese School by such artists as Sassetta, Sano di Pietro, Giovanni di Paolo and their followers. The design seems to have had a long period of currency for its first appearance is in the early 14th century and the last, in slightly altered form, in an *Adoration of the Child* by Sano di Pietro (Kress Collection, Washington, D.C.) probably of the 1470s. All are shown as large borderless floor-carpets and there are sometimes indications of a very coarsely knotted texture. The origin of these pieces, and of similar ones showing animals with their heads and tails turned inwards, is still uncertain. No fragment of them has ever been found in Turkey itself or elsewhere for the comparisons which have been made of them with some surviving Near Eastern rugs and fragments cannot be sustained. We thus do not know even in what technique they were made and their place of origin is wholly conjectural. There do exist certain Turkish rugs with bird-like forms stylized in a completely different way – the famous Marby rug (no. 2) and a carpet still in Konya in which the field is decorated with many birds – and this type does seem to be represented in several paintings by the Catalan artist Jaime Huguet.

Still another type of animal design is found in the dragon-and-phoenix rugs of the 15th century. The best, and most famous, representation of one of these is Domenico di Bartolo's fresco *The Marriage of the Foundlings* in the Hospital of Sta. Maria della Scala in Siena. The carpet in this is particularly close to a fragment, once in the Cairo art market, described by Erdmann.[9] Another painting, one of the *Scenes from the Life of St. Vincent Ferrer* by Bartolommeo degli Erri (fig. 5), shows a small rug of this type hanging from a window-sill. Because they relate closely to later geometrical Turkish rugs there is good reason to think that these were indeed pieces imported from Turkey.

5 Bartolommeo degli Erri,
Scenes from the Life of St. Vincent Ferrer (detail), second half fifteenth century, with dragon-and-phoenix rug.
Kunsthistorisches Museum, Vienna.

6 Florentine School, *Cassone Panel with a Battle Scene* (detail), second half fifteenth century, showing carpets with heraldic designs, perhaps of local manufacture.
Courtauld Institute Galleries, University of London (Gambier-Parry Collection).

At the same time as this, however, there appear in Florentine paintings, particularly those on the sides of *cassone*
(large wedding chests) small rugs with both geometrical and
animal designs, the latter stylized in curious, starkly geometrical ways. They are all quite different from the large
carpets shown in the Sienese paintings and are used differently
– hanging from window-sills, for example, from which
ladies and gentlemen look out on to tournament scenes or
other activities. Some of them show what look like heraldic
motifs (fig. 6) which are, occasionally, recognizable as belonging to particular families. It does seem quite likely
therefore that these small rugs were of local manufacture.
We cannot say with certainty that they were piled rugs but
usually they do at least show a fringe, that is the ends of the
warp threads.

The foregoing carpets are mostly rather problematical as
regards place of origin but their appearances serve equally
with the later to indicate to us how carpets were used in the
Italy of the 14th to 16th centuries. Large carpets were used
on the floor for special occasions such as weddings; they are
also to be seen on the floor in scenes of the Annunciation,
the Virgin being seated either directly on one or, perhaps
more likely, on a low stool or cushion, and this presumably
reflects usage in a gentlewoman's bedroom or chamber.
Small rugs certainly were used in bedrooms at the side or
foot of the bed; they so appear in paintings, and inventories
refer specifically to such use, for example '*uno tappeto da
tenere a pie del letto . . .* ' (1418).[10] They were also used on
tables and desks, and on benches. Their use for purposes of
display, hanging from window-sills, has been noted on the
cassone panels of Florence and was to become even more
characteristic of Venice as seen especially in the paintings of
Carpaccio and Mansueti. The *St. Ursula Cycle* of the former
is particularly notable in this respect (front endpaper). On
public occasions use of a carpet reflected the dignity and

authority of whoever might have it before him on a table or,
even more so, at his feet. Conversely such usage also conferred
dignity and honour and so was not to be lightly assumed by
those not entitled to it. The carpet at the feet of the Madonna
and Child Enthroned must reflect such usage by popes,
doges, and other rulers; that invariably present on the table
in paintings showing The Calling of Matthew[11] must be in-
dicative of the practice of such officials as tax-collectors.

Beginning in the middle of the 15th century, and so over-
lapping to some extent with the appearances of animal-design
carpets, the Italian paintings began to show well-known
types of geometrical-design Ottoman carpets of which many
examples have survived. In the early days of carpet studies
names had to be found to distinguish the various designs
pending a more logical nomenclature based on the yet to be
discovered places of origin. Names of painters who depicted
them were therefore used purely as a convenience but these
names have tended to stick and indeed to be added to in
recent years. The large-pattern Holbeins, named after the
rug in that artist's '*The Ambassadors*' (fig. 7), are among the
earliest to be seen. These probably do not form a single
group: certainly there exists more than one design scheme
but the most familiar is one with octagons ('wheels') within large rectangles. These seem to be closely related to
the earlier dragon-and-phoenix rugs and certain other surviving rugs which include stylized animals. An early appearance (1468) is in Marco Costanzo's *St. Gerolamo* in the
cathedral in Syracuse; another is in Antonello da Messina's
St. Sebastian (1476) in Dresden. Crivelli's *Annunciation*
(1486), in the National Gallery, London, has a good example
while some appear in Carpaccio's paintings mentioned
above. Another form appears in a *Madonna and Child* of
c.1484 by Ghirlandaio (Uffizi, Florence) and also, though
less completely, in Mantegna's frescos in the *Camera degli
Sposi* in the Ducal Palace in Mantua. There are many other
examples and the design continues to appear throughout the
next century in paintings by, for example, the Cremonese
artist Sofonisba Anguissola. In the 17th century it is still
occasionally to be seen in paintings of the English and
Dutch schools.

Despite the name the small-pattern Holbeins have no
obvious relationship to the preceding type though they
appear at about the same time or slightly earlier. The first to
be seen in a painting is that in the much damaged fresco of
1451 by Piero della Francesca in S. Francesco, Rimini while
shortly after (1459) there is that in Mantegna's *Madonna
and Child* in the church of S. Zeno in Verona. A strikingly
painted example is in the anonymous *Madonna and Child
with Sts. Leonardo and Giovanni* in the Museo Nazionale di
Capodimonte in Naples, and another in a beautiful *Annunciation* of about 1508 by Andrea Previtali (fig. 8). In fact
over fifty occurrences have been noted,[12] mostly in Italian
paintings, the peak period being the first quarter of the 16th
century. They do not appear in Italian paintings after the
middle of the century and seem to have gone out of favour.

An early type of Turkish rug design which has received
much less attention than the above two is that of the prayer
rugs variously referred to as 'keyhole', 're-entrant', or 'Bellini'
rugs.[13] These include in their design an infolding of the
inner border or stripe to give an octagonal niche at one end.
This may be repeated at the other end but more commonly
there is a pointed arch, perhaps with hanging lamps. In
paintings usually only one end is shown and one cannot
know about the other. Notable examples of this type of rug

7 Hans Holbein the Younger,
Jean de Dinteville and George de Selve ('*The Ambassadors*')
(detail), 1533.
Reproduced by courtesy of the Trustees of the National Gallery,
London.

8 Andrea Previtali, *Annunciation* (detail), *c.* 1508,
   showing a small-pattern Holbein carpet.
   Church of Sta. Maria in Meschio, Vittorio Veneto.

9 Garofalo (attributed),
   ceiling fresco (detail), first half 16th century,
   showing 'Bellini' rug.
   Palace of Lodovico il Moro, Ferrara.

10 Francesco Bassano il Vecchio,
Madonna and Child Enthroned, 1519,
showing 'keyhole' or 're-entrant' rug.
Museo Civico, Bassano del Grappa.

10a Francesco Bassano il Vecchio,
Madonna and Child Enthroned (detail), 1519,
showing 'keyhole' or 're-entrant' rug.
Museo Civico, Bassano del Grappa.

occur in the *Madonna and Child* of 1493 by Cima in the cathedral of Conegliano, and in the delightful ceiling fresco, perhaps by Garofalo, in the Palace of Lodovico il Moro in Ferrara (fig. 9) which shows eight carpets hanging from a balcony. Lorenzo Lotto shows this type three times: two are rather similar, in a *Madonna and Child* of 1507 in Sta. Cristina al Tivarone, Treviso and another in Sto. Spirito in Bergamo. The third, in a *Double Portrait* in the Hermitage, Leningrad, has a 'ragged palmette' border and comes closer to most surviving pieces. Another very clear example is in a *Madonna and Child Enthroned* of 1519 by Francesco Bassano il Vecchio (figs. 10, 10a). The name 'Bellini' comes from the appearance of the top end of one of these rugs in a painting of the *Virgin and Child Enthroned* by Gentile Bellini in the National Gallery, London as well as another one in *The Doge Loredan and Four Advisers* by (in part) Giovanni Bellini, last seen in a sale in Munich in 1931.[14]

The small-pattern Holbein rugs were apparently displaced in popularity in Italy by the 'arabesque Ushak' or 'Lotto' rugs, of more stereotyped design and colouring. The first certain depiction of one of these is in a painting of *Cardinal Bandinello Sauli*, of 1516, by Sebastiano del Piombo in Washington, D.C., and appearances reach their peak in the second quarter of the century. These earlier examples mostly have forms of Kufic border (like the small-pattern Holbeins before them), usually in white on a green ground. Good examples occur in an anonymous painting of *Cardinal Marcello Cervini* in the Galleria Borghese, Rome, and in a *Madonna and Child Enthroned* by Benedetto Carpaccio in the cathedral of Koper, Yugoslavia (formerly Capodistria). This last is in the 'kilim' style,[15] less common in these early pieces than in those of the next century. The two examples in paintings by Lotto himself are in the *Family Group*, in the National Gallery, London, and the *Sant'Antonino Elemosinario* in Venice (fig. 11). As already noted, Lotto shows other types of rug also, but it seems that his name will now always be associated with these supposedly Ushak pieces. It has often been wondered whether artists owned the carpets they depicted. In the case of Lotto this can partly be answered: he did own at least one though we cannot say of which type it was. He kept careful account of all his financial transactions and his account book, the *Libro di Spese Diverse*, has survived and been published.[16] One entry records his pawning a carpet: ' . . . *un tapedo turchesco da mastabe alto di pelo et forma largo . . .*' (a Turkish carpet for a bench of good pile and large size), together with another article, for three ducats. Three months later he records their recovery on payment of the capital and interest.

In the second half of the century representation of carpets in paintings becomes rather sparse but 'Lottos' continue to be seen, now however usually with different border systems such as forms of meander. An unusual and otherwise unknown border appears early in the next century, incorporating the arms of the Milanese Crespi family, in G. B. Crespi's *The Miracle of Beatrice Crespi* in Milan.

Other groups of rugs which are also usually ascribed to the Ushak district are also to be seen in 16th century Italian paintings. One of the double-niche or small medallion Ushak rugs is to be seen already by 1519 in Gerolamo da Santacroce's *The Calling of Matthew* in Bassano. This has a cloud-band border, also present on similar rugs in a *Portrait of a Lady* by Francesco Vecellio (Titian's brother) of 1561 (fig. 12) and *The Honesty of St. Eligius* of 1614 by Jacopo Chimenti, 'L'Empoli', in the Uffizi. The white ground rugs, also often

11 Lorenzo Lotto, *Sant' Antonino Elemosinario*.
The two carpets shown are an arabesque Ushak or 'Lotto' rug, and a para-Mamluk.
Church of Sts. Giovanni e Paolo, Venice

having cloud-band borders, are rather rarely seen in paintings, indeed the Chintamani design of three balls and wavy lines has not been noticed at all. One of the 'bird' rugs is to be seen in a male portrait ascribed to G. B. Moroni (present whereabouts unknown) while a later example occurs in the *Eumenius and Roxane* of Alessandro Varotari, 'il Padovanino', in the Hermitage. The large star and medallion Ushaks are particularly rare. The former occurs once quite early, in 1534, in Paris Bordone's *Return of the Ring to the Doge* (Accademia, Venice) and is then not noticed again until it appears in an 18th century work. The medallion Ushaks do not get a showing at all until they are seen in some paintings of the second half of the 17th century by the Bergamese still-life artists Evaristo Baschenis, Bartolommeo Bettera and their followers.

All the above are undoubtedly Anatolian carpets but there are also appearances, albeit somewhat rare ones, of pieces from elsewhere, as well as those whose place of origin is still undecided. The Mamluk carpets of Egypt make scattered appearances throughout the 16th century, suggesting continued production rather later than used to be thought. Nearly all are in Venetian or north Italian paintings, the earliest being a second carpet in the now lost Giovanni Bellini painting of *c*.1507 referred to above. The latest are several examples in the works of Leandro Bassano from the end of the century. Particularly good, and painted in amazing detail for fresco, are some in wall-paintings in the Martinengo-Salvadego Palace in Brescia, of before 1543, which are attributed to School or follower of Moretto (back endpaper). They show young ladies of the family behind parapets, over which are draped a number of Mamluk rugs of different designs. Related to the Mamluks by having a number of design elements in common with them are the 'para-Mamluks' and their successors the 'compartment' rugs. The earliest appearance of one of these is in a painting of 1501 by Giovanni Martine da Udine, *St. Mark Enthroned with Saints*, but there is reason to think they came to Italy at least fifty years earlier. An inventory of St. Peter's in Rome of 1455 mentions four rugs, one being described as having a large central medallion surrounded by four small medallions, 'and with darts'.[17] This sounds like a succinct description of the usual para-Mamluk design though it could fit, less aptly, some Mamluks. Two paintings by Lotto show this type of carpet but around the middle of the century it is replaced by the compartment rugs which continue into the 17th century.

And what of carpets from Persia? Did none come to Italy during the 16th century? There is very little evidence from the paintings that they did, though there do appear a very few carpets with floral designs which it is difficult to be certain about. One is in Paris Bordone's *Chess Players* of the mid-century in Berlin, but this may, rather, be one of the Ottoman court carpets, not otherwise noticed. At the end of the century a Persian product is certainly shown in Leandro Bassano's *Portrait of a Senator* (fig. 13). It is not a pile rug but a well-known type of silk kilim, produced probably under the patronage of Shah Abbas and sent by him among gifts carried by diplomatic missions. This is very probably how this particular example arrived in Venice.

12 Francesco Vecellio, *Portrait of a Lady*, 1561,
showing double-niche Ushak rug with cloud-band border.
Formerly Holford Collection, London.

13 Leandro Bassano, *Portrait of a Senator*,
last quarter 16th century, showing Persian silk kilim of the
Shah Abbas period.
Ashmolean Museum, Oxford.

14 Hans Eworth (attributed), *King Henry VIII*,
second quarter 16th century, showing a star Ushak carpet.
Walker Art Gallery, Liverpool.

Carpets in England

It was most probably via Italy, and more particularly Venice,
that Near Eastern carpets first came to England. The first
we hear of them is the saga of Cardinal Wolsey's efforts to
obtain some.[18] The story has been often told but bears
repeating. The details were recorded by the Venetian ambassador, Sebastiano Giustiniani, in his dispatches home.
In June 1518 the Venetian traders in London appealed to
Wolsey for help in obtaining the repeal of the duties on
Candian wines, which they imported into England. After
their conversation on this topic the Cardinal in turn appealed
to the merchants to obtain some carpets for him which he
said he would pay for. Only in November did the merchants
make him an offer of seven carpets which Wolsey however,
who had been offended by real or imagined slights on their
part, only agreed to accept as a joint gift of the ambassador
and the merchants. This was not enough, it seems, for a year
later the affair of the duties on the wine was still unsettled
and the ambassador reported back to the Venetian Senate
that the Cardinal had asked several times for a hundred
carpets, which he urged should be sent. A year later still, in
October 1520, Wolsey received sixty carpets from Venice.
The story well illustrates the extreme scarcity of such carpets
at the time. Wolsey was immensely rich and in power only
second to the king, yet it took him over two years to obtain
them. In 1528 he fell from favour and forfeited all his goods
to the king, presumably his carpets among them for this was
no matter just of form. He had to live for several weeks at
Esher without crockery and bedlinen until, on appeal, some
were returned to him. Henry VIII certainly owned large

numbers of carpets at his death in 1547. They were distrib-
uted between his many houses and palaces, and the entries
in the inventories which refer to them have very recently
been published in full.[19] More than half of the eight hundred
entries refer to carpets of 'Turkey making'. While there is no
indication of the techniques of these it is a reasonable
assumption that they were knotted pile carpets. The inventories also indicate the uses to which the carpets were put
and include 'foot carpets'. Some, indeed, were so large that
they could hardly have been used otherwise than on the
floor. Henry is usually shown in paintings standing (fig. 14)
or enthroned upon a carpet and, when these are recognizable,
they are usually in Turkish or Turkish-inspired designs.
When the painter is Holbein, as in the fresco in Whitehall
Palace of which a 17th century copy remains (the palace
itself was destroyed by fire in 1698) we can be confident as to
the accuracy of the depiction, but in the many near-contem-
porary replicas based only loosely on Holbein's work we can
be less sure. Curious features of some of the carpets shown
in these may be due to artistic incompetence or, possibly, to
the fact that the carpets themselves were not Turkish but

English-made copies. Such were certainly made for there are many references to them in the inventories. Also some have survived though not from quite as early as this. At all events it seems that the types which Henry possessed included: large-pattern Holbeins, 'Lottos', star and medallion Ushaks and their variants, double-niche Ushaks, and the white ground Chintamani rugs. This last type is recognizable from the inventory descriptions though it has not been noticed in the paintings. Henry must also have owned small-pattern Holbeins since a year or two after his death his son, the young King Edward VI (fig. 15), is shown standing on a very beautiful example with green ground and brilliant colours and having medallions with the unusual quartered colouring.

Although distressingly many of Henry's carpets are de-

scribed already in the inventories as moth-eaten and full of holes (conditions in his palaces, often empty and neglected when he was not there, must have been inimical to sound conservation) most of them will have continued in royal possession until sold off by the Commonwealth after the execution of Charles I in 1649. Elizabeth's interest in carpets, if any, is undocumented and she is rarely shown with one. However one painting does show her standing on a carpet, interestingly one of the rather rare compartment carpets. It was in the first two decades of the 17th century, under James I, that carpets became an indispensable adjunct of the standing portrait. The King himself is several times shown standing on one (often of floral design and probably Persian) but more interesting are their appearances in portraits of dignitaries and noblemen by several artists, above all William Larkin. He must himself have owned carpets since the same design appears in several portraits as a kind of prop.[20] In these portraits we see compartment carpets (apparently: only the border is shown), 'Lottos', large-pattern Holbeins, and a curious rug with animal-like motifs which seem to hark back to the dragon-and-phoenix rugs. There are no small-pattern Holbeins; output of these must have ceased some time before as noticed already in regard to the Italian paintings. The large example in *The Somerset House Conference, 1604* (cover) must have been already old at the time: perhaps it was one of Henry's pieces. Incidentally, use of carpets on a table used for writing, as in this painting, had its

15 Unknown artist, *King Edward VI, c.* 1550,
    showing small-pattern Holbein carpet.
    Reproduced by permission of the Trustees of the
    National Portrait Gallery, London.

16 Michiel Janszoon van Miereveld, *Prince Rupert*, 1625,
   showing a double-niche Ushak rug.
   Reproduced by gracious permission of Her Majesty The Queen.

predictable accidents: one in the inventories is described as 'steyned with yncke'. By the time of Charles I familiarity with the old Turkish carpets in the royal collection may have made them begin to seem rather old-fashioned. The Royal Family is usually shown (especially by van Dyck) in association with carpets in the Herat design and so either Persian or Indian. There is however a delightful portrait of *Prince Rupert*, dated 1625, by Miereveld (fig. 16) which shows him standing on a small, probably almost new, double-niche Ushak rug.

Carpets in Spain

The carpets of Spain were mentioned earlier but nothing was said as to their use in Spain and appearances in Spanish painting. There is nothing so early as the Avignon fresco but in the 15th century there are a few examples. A painting of *St. George with a Banner*, of the Catalan Aragonese School in the Art Institute of Chicago shows a carpet in the large-pattern Holbein design. Although Spanish rugs were made in this design it seems more likely that this is actually a Turkish example.[21] An unknown Castilian painter of the end of the century in his *St. Anne Enthroned with the Virgin and Child* (The Metropolitan Museum of Art, New York) shows what must be a Spanish carpet with Kufic border and a simple field design of swastikas in squares. Early in the

17 Alonso de Sedano,
The Miracle of Sts. Cosmas and Damian, early 16th century, showing a Spanish carpet with European design.
Wellcome Institute Library, London.

16th century Alonso de Sedano's *Miracle of Sts. Cosmas and Damian* (fig. 17) shows a carpet with a now non-Turkish design with a diagonal trellis, but the Kufic-inspired border remains. As to Spanish carpets elsewhere in Europe, there is the appearance in a miniature in a manuscript of the third quarter of the 15th century (Hofbibliotek, Vienna) of a 'Cuenca' carpet with the Spanish version of the 'Lotto' design. This appearance, well before the known production of the Turkish version, has not been adequately accounted for. A remarkable representation of a Spanish rug comes in Holbein's *Madonna and Child with two Saints* (the *Solothurn Madonna*) of 1522. This shows the arms of the Gerster family of Basle and has a border perfectly characteristic of the armorial design, or admiral's carpets. It must have been made to order in Spain. Much later, in 1639, the newly appointed Spanish governor-general of the Netherlands (which returned to Spanish dominion in 1633), the Cardinal-Infant Ferdinand, was portrayed by the Antwerp artist Gaspar de Crayer (the painting is in the Prado, Madrid) standing on a Spanish carpet of the period which he must have brought with him from Spain. At this period Spanish painters seem more usually to show Turkish rugs. Murillo shows 'Lottos' as does Zurbarán, who also adds star and medallion Ushaks.

Carpets in northern Europe

It was in northern Europe, particularly in the Holland of the 17th century, that Near Eastern carpets were to achieve the peak of their popularity. They are already to be seen in the first half of the 15th century in the paintings of Jan van Eyck and Petrus Christus but the designs shown, a bold geometric trellis containing knots or stars, or large eight-pointed stars, do not correspond to anything known in surviving carpets and so it is uncertain where they were made. In the second half of the century rather similar designs are seen in the paintings of Gerard David but it was above all Hans Memling who gave us the most complete survey of the sorts of carpet available at that time. Several of those which he shows come close to the large-pattern Holbeins in their octagon in a rectangle arrangement and the decorative filling of the octagons is also often similar. Another field pattern commonly seen is a repeat of medallions with hooked outlines (fig. 18). These have recently started to be referred to as 'Memling guls' in descriptions of 19th and 20th century Caucasian, Turkish, and Kurdish rugs on which they often appear. It is in the borders that Memling's rug designs often differ rather markedly from known early Turkish pieces. Several show a chevron pattern and often the corners of the main border are divided off as squares containing a star or other motif which may be different from those in the border itself. This was not known in Turkish rugs until recently when it was noticed on one, probably of the late 18th century.[22]

In the 16th century paintings from northern Europe showing carpets are rather scarce despite the famous occurrences in those of Hans Holbein in the 3rd and 4th decades. Earlier than Holbein however there were some equally careful depictions: that of The Master of St. Giles in *The Mass of St. Giles* of around 1500 (fig. 19) being probably the most meticulous of all, and there is another large-pattern Holbein in the Cologne School *Altarpiece of the Holy Kindred* of similar date (Wallraf-Richartz Museum, Cologne). Bernard van Orley, in a *Holy Family* of 1522 (Prado, Madrid) shows a fine green-ground small-pattern Holbein. In the middle of the century Flemish paintings start to show a few rugs in domestic contexts. Willem Key in *Portraits of the Smit Family* (Brussels, Musée d'Art Ancien) carefully shows a part of an Ushak rug, probably a star Ushak. In 1561 Frans Floris, in his painting of the *van Berchem Family*[23] (Lier, Wuyts van Campen en Baron Caroly Museum) shows a 'Lotto' with white on green Kufic border similar to those to be seen in Italian and Portuguese paintings of the first half of the century. A similar *Family Portrait*, of 1564, by Cornelis de Zeeuw (fig. 20) also shows an Ushak rug, of uncertain type, with a cloud-band border. Generally though this seems a depressed period: it was only after the first independence of Holland from Spain in 1609 and its freedom to pursue its own way and its own trade that a burgeoning middle-class life created a great demand for luxury goods such as carpets and also for paintings. Many of the numerous carpets shown in Dutch paintings throughout this century are still Turkish. How these came to Holland is not known exactly: probably many came overland or up the Danube to Germany. 'Lotto' carpets appear throughout the century though now with different borders from those of the previous one, usually of the cartouche (fig. 21) or cloud-band types. Next most frequent are the so-called 'Transylvanians' (fig. 22). These appear to have come on the European scene only in this century but then continue to appear occasionally in paintings, in a progressively changing style, through the 18th century and into the early 19th. A few examples of other Turkish types are also seen: one or two large-pattern Holbeins, still quite similar to the 15th century designs; double-niche Ushaks; medallion Ushaks; the occasional compartment carpet.

18 Hans Memling, *Madonna and Child Enthroned* (detail), showing unusual Turkish rug of 'Memling' type. Musée du Louvre, Paris.

19 The Master of St. Giles, *The Mass of St. Giles*, c. 1500 (detail), showing large-pattern Holbein rug. Reproduced by courtesy of the Trustees of the National Gallery, London.

20 Cornelis de Zeeuw, *Family Portrait*, 1564 (detail), showing an Ushak rug of uncertain type with cloud-band border. Westfälisches Landesmuseum, für Kunst und Kultergeschichte, Münster.

22 Pieter Codde, *La Toilette*,
showing a Transylvanian rug.
Musée du Louvre, Paris.

24 Pieter Anraedt, *Six Regents and the Housemaster of
the Oude Zijds Institute for the Outdoor Relief of the Poor,
Amsterdam*, 1675 (detail),
showing a Herat carpet.
Historisches Museum, Amsterdam.

The Dutch East India Company was formed in 1602 and
it is not surprising that large numbers of 'Indo-Isfahan'
carpets are shown in the paintings. Sufficient study has not
yet been given to these to determine which exactly are of
Indian and which of Persian manufacture. Even when Persian
they were probably often brought overland to India and
then by sea. They are to be seen already quite early in the
century in the work of Rubens, later very frequently in the
work of Gaspar de Crayer as well as numerous Dutch genre
painters up into the 18th century. We see from these latter
artists how familiar an item the carpet was becoming by now
in scenes of domestic life and activities, as some titles
sufficiently indicate: *A Musical Party*; *The Music Lesson*;
The Visit of the Doctor; *Lady and Maid Feeding a Parrot*; *A
Lady at her Toilet*; *Dutch Courtship*. In all these a carpet
covers the table. When the 'courtship' turns into 'merry
company' – or more frankly a brothel scene – the carpet may
be rather rumpled (fig. 23).

The carpet as status symbol survives in the numerous –
sometimes they seem to be almost annual – paintings of
boards of governors of charities, hospitals, prisons etc. which
were produced for a hundred years or more. These usually
display a particularly large and grand carpet on the table
around which are seated the gentlemen, and sometimes
ladies, of the board attended by their steward. Herat or
Indo-Isfahan carpets predominate here (fig. 24), sometimes

21 Salomon Mesdach, *Willem Courten (1581–1630)*, 1617,
showing a Lotto rug with cartouche border.
Rijksmuseum, Amsterdam.

23 Jacob Duck, *Merry Company* (detail),
    showing a 'Lotto' rug with cartouche border.
    Musée du Louvre on loan to Musée des Beaux-Arts, Nîmes.

showing heraldic blazons which would suggest that they
were made to order. Towards the end of the 17th century
another type of Ushak carpet makes its appearance, the
Smyrna design or floral Ushaks, rather coarse derivatives of
the Ottoman court carpet designs.

Use of the carpet on the floor still seems to be relatively
uncommon in the ordinary household until towards the end
of the century. In a painting of 1687 by Michiel van Musscher
(fig. 25) we see Thomas Hees, returned from his duties in
Algeria, Tunis and Tripoli, well attended and making himself very comfortable with what looks like a Persian 'vase'
carpet on his table and an Ushak 'Smyrna' carpet on the
floor. So it was to be for the future, for during the 18th
century, in a household of any pretensions, a carpeted floor
was to become the rule rather than the exception.

25 Michiel van Musscher,
    Thomas Hees with his Nephews and Negro Servant, 1687 (detail).
    The carpet on the table resembles a Persian 'Vase' carpet in
    some particulars; that on the floor is a 'Smyrna' or floral
    Ushak carpet.
    Rijksmuseum, Amsterdam.

1. These were resumed in A. U. Dilley (revised by M. S. Dimand),
    Oriental Rugs and Carpets, Philadelphia and New York, 1959; more
    recently, and in the light of later knowledge, by R. Pinner, 'The
    earliest carpets', *Hali*, 5 (1982), pp. 111–15.
2. S. I. Rudenko, *Frozen Tombs of Siberia – the Pazyryk Burials of Iron
    Age Horsemen*, London, 1970.
3. M. S. Dimand, 'An early cut-pile rug from Egypt', *Metropolitan
    Museum Studies*, 4 (1933), p. 151 ff.
4. Jean Ebersolt, *Les Arts Somptuaires de Byzance*, Paris, 1923, p. 147.
5. The Arab geographer El-Edrisi says: 'In Chinchilla are made woollen
    carpets which cannot be imitated elsewhere'. The Arab writer Al-
    Saqundi says of Murcia: 'It is also celebrated for the carpets of al-
    Tantaliya (Chinchilla?) which are exported to all countries of East and
    West'. As cited in J. Ferrandis Torres, *Alfombras Antiguas Españolas*,
    Madrid, 1933, pp. 27–8.
6. Illustrated in E. de Lorey, 'Le Tapis d'Avignon', *Gazette des Beaux-
    Arts*, 6ème période, T.8 (1932), pp. 162–71.
7. Iris Origo, *The Merchant of Prato*, London, 1957.
8. First studied in detail by K. Erdmann, 'Orientalische Tierteppiche
    auf Bildern des XIV und XV Jahrhunderts', *Jahrbuch der Preussischen
    Kunstsammlungen*, 50 (1929), p. 261–98; 'Neue Orientalische
    Tierteppiche auf Abendlandischen Bildern des XIV und XV
    Jahrhunderts', *ibid.*, 63 (1942), pp. 121–6. See also J. Mills, 'Early
    animal carpets in Western paintings', *Hali*, 1 (1978), pp. 234–43.
9. K. Erdmann, 'Zu einem Anatolischen Teppichfragment aus Fostat',
    Istanbuler Mitteilungen, 6 (1955), pp. 41–51.
10. A. Schiaparelli, *La Casa Fiorentina e i suoi Arredi*, Florence, 1908,
    p. 224, note 8.
11. This may be seen in paintings of different schools over at least three
    hundred years, from that of Andrea and Jacopo di Cione of 1367–70
    (Uffizi, Florence) to Juan de Pareja's of 1661 (Prado, Madrid).
12. J. Mills, 'Small-pattern Holbein carpets in Western paintings', *Hali*, 1
    (1978), pp. 326–34; C. G. Ellis, 'Small-pattern Holbein carpets in
    Western paintings – a continuation', *Hali*, 3 (1980), pp. 216–17.
13. Many of the paintings showing this design have been enumerated and
    studied by J. Zick, 'Eine Gruppe von Gebetsteppichen und ihre
    Datierung', *Berliner Museen, Berichte aus den ehem. Preuss.
    Kunstsammlungen*, Neue Folge, Jg. 11 (1961), pp. 6–14.
14. Nemes Sale, Munich, 16.6.31, lot 24.
15. The various styles of drafting the 'Lotto' pattern were first described
    by C. G. Ellis, 'The "Lotto" pattern as a fashion in carpets', *Festschrift
    für Peter Wilhelm Meister*, Hamburg, 1975, pp. 19–31.
16. P. Zampetti, editor, *Libro di Spese Diverse*, Venice, 1963. I have
    quoted the excerpt in greater length in 'I Tappeti medio-orientali
    nella pittura italiana', in *Il tappeto orientale dal XV al XVIII secolo*,
    Eskenazi, Milan, 1981, and I am indebted to Miss J. Plesters for
    bringing it to my attention.
17. '*rubeum cum una rosa in medio magna et quattuor rosis aliis parvis
    circumspica et cum spicis*'. E. Müntz and A. L. Frothingham, *Il tesoro
    della basilica di S. Pietro in Vaticano dal XIII al XV secolo con una
    scelta d'inventari inediti*, Rome, 1893, p. 125. I am much indebted to
    Mr. J. Michael Rogers for this information.
18. A. F. Kendrick and C. E. C. Tattersall, *Hand-Woven Carpets*,
    London, 1922, pp. 76–7.
19. D. King, 'The inventories of the carpets of King Henry VIII', *Hali*, 5
    (1983), pp. 287–96.
20. R. Strong, *The English Icon: Elizabethan and Jacobean Portraiture*,
    London, 1969.
21. Louise Mackie, 'Native and foreign influences in carpets woven in
    Spain during the 15th century', *Hali*, 2 (1979), pp. 88–95.
22. T. Stauffer, 'A central Anatolian rug with a 15th century design',
    Hali, 4 (1982), p. 365.
23. Illustrated in colour in J. Mills, '"Lotto" carpets in Western
    paintings', *Hali*, 3 (1981), pp. 278–89.

The Carpets in the Exhibition

Donald King

The exhibition, *The Eastern Carpet in the Western World from the 15th to the 17th century*, aims to provide, within a limited space, a reasonably comprehensive view of the kinds of carpets which were imported into Europe and which carried a wealth of Oriental design and colour into the homes, the daily life and the artistic consciousness of Europeans in the Renaissance and Baroque periods. Naturally, carpets made between three and six centuries ago are rare, precious and in many cases extremely frail. Thus some examples which one would have dearly liked to include cannot be exposed to the risks of travel. But the great museums of the world and the major private collectors have responded with extraordinary generosity to requests for the loan of some of their greatest treasures, so that the display not only offers a marvellous survey of the best in Oriental carpet design from the 15th to the 17th century, but also gives the public a unique opportunity of seeing a number of carpets of the highest importance which are little known, and some which have never previously been exhibited.

It would have been appropriate, if it were possible, to show only carpets which are known to have arrived in Europe soon after they were made, but the evidence is insufficient to make an exhibition entirely on this basis. We can be sure of the fact mainly in the case of carpets in the Oriental style which were actually made in Europe, by the old-established carpet workshops of Spain (nos. 3–5, 7, 13), or the newer ones in England (nos. 33, 37) and in Poland (no. 42). Among carpets made in the east, some of the most reliable evidence is that of carpets with coats of arms, which must have been specially commissioned from the Oriental carpet weaving centres by the families concerned (figs. 35, 36; no. 73). It is only extremely rarely that existing Oriental carpets can actually be identified in contemporary European documents, as is the case of the two extraordinary, newly discovered Cairene carpets from the Pitti Palace, which are recorded in the inventories of the Medici Grand Dukes in the 16th and 17th centuries (nos. 21, 56). Even without documentary proof, it is very probable that carpets from old European collections, such as the Imperial Collection in Vienna (nos. 22, 58) and the Swedish Royal Collections (no. 65), or from European churches (nos. 1, 2, 79) or great houses such as Hardwick and Boughton (nos. 32, 36, 70) have been in Europe for several centuries. This is also quite likely for pieces from museum collections such as those of Budapest, which are largely drawn from church and lay collections in areas of Europe which lay within, or on the fringes of, the territory of the Ottoman empire at the relevant period (nos. 11, 14, 15, 34, 47, 48). Most of the carpets shown, however, have a known history which extends no further back than the past fifty to a hundred years, so that

we cannot be absolutely sure that these individual pieces reached Europe at the time of manufacture. What we can be quite sure of, however, is that carpets like these were used in Europe, because exactly similar carpets are seen in European paintings. Paintings are indeed a primary source for the history of Oriental carpets in Europe; the theme of carpets in paintings has been explored by John Mills in an essay in this catalogue and in a separate exhibition at the National Gallery this summer. While nearly all the carpets in the present exhibition are either known to have been in Europe since the relevant period, or belong to types which are known to have been current in Europe at the time, a few pieces have been included, not for their European connections, but because they help to illustrate and define the character and interaction of the various traditions of carpet designing and carpet weaving in the many different centres, extending from Spain in the west to India in the east, which supplied their products to the European market.

The historical background

Imports of Oriental carpets were by no means a novelty in the Renaissance. The discovery of the famous carpet from Pazyryk, made between the 5th and the 3rd centuries BC, leaves little room for doubt that some of the carpets mentioned by classical authors must have been Oriental knotted pile carpets. It is almost axiomatic, though documentary evidence is wanting, that the Byzantine Empire, which controlled large areas of the Near East, must have been amply provided with carpets. Throughout the Middle Ages western Europe received supplies of silk textiles from Asia and it is virtually certain that a number of carpets must have come with them. Western Crusaders in the Near East were presumably acquainted with carpets and brought some home. By the late 12th century there is evidence for the export of some sort of carpets from the Muslim areas of southern Spain and there are important remains of a large pictorial carpet made at that time in Germany. It is, however, possible that knotted carpets remained relatively rare in Europe. In the 14th century Italian paintings begin to provide abundant evidence of patterned floor-coverings, but it is by no means certain that these were Oriental knotted-pile carpets. It is only from the 15th century onwards that we are able to follow in considerable detail, from paintings and from surviving pieces, the arrival in Europe of many different types of Oriental carpet.

Europe had a long history of hostilities with the carpet-producing areas, alternating with occupation of parts of them. The Greeks had fought with the Persians and eventually, under Alexander, occupied their territory. The Romans and Byzantines fought with the Parthians and Sassanians, while remaining in possession of much of the Near East. In the 7th and 8th centuries Arab armies, inspired by the aggressive faith of Islam, seized much of the Near East, overran Sassanian Persia and advanced along the North African coast, through Spain and into France, where they were finally halted at Tours and Poitiers in 732. There followed several centuries of relative equilibrium, punctuated by many wars. The Muslims were gradually pressed back into southern Spain, whence they were not finally expelled until 1492. Western Crusaders launched attacks on the Near East, but these weakened Byzantium more than Islam. On the other hand, Muslim strength was temporarily shattered by the assaults of the Mongols in the 13th and 14th centuries. During the 14th and 15th centuries a new aggressive Islamic power, that of the Ottoman Turks, grew up in Anatolia and occupied the residue of Byzantine territory there and in south-eastern Europe; Constantinople fell in 1453. Italy was shocked by the Ottoman occupation of Otranto in 1480. In 1516–17 the Ottomans broke the Mamluk dynasty and occupied Syria and Egypt. Hungary fell into their hands in 1526 and Vienna was besieged in 1529. Extensive areas of north-west Persia were occupied and vassal states were set up along the North African coast as far as Algiers. During the second half of the 16th century the Ottoman advance was halted; their siege of Malta failed in 1565 and in 1571 the battle of Lepanto broke their naval dominance in the Mediterranean. Meanwhile, in the east, the Safavid Shahs of Persia stabilized their frontiers with the Turks and established a prosperous economy, while northern India was dominated by the rich and powerful Mughal dynasty. In the 17th century the Turks launched further assaults on central Europe, which finally failed at the siege of Vienna in 1683, whereafter they were gradually forced back throughout south-eastern Europe.

This vertiginously foreshortened view of history offers a perspective of conflicts and battles which is wholly misleading. Of course the opposition between west and east, between Christian and Islamic powers, was an historical fact which had endless repercussions in politics and affairs of state. But the essence of the situation was not conflict, but co-existence. The frontiers between the two sides were never closed or watertight. Diplomacy bridged them easily. To combat the Ottoman Turks Venice sought an alliance with the Turkomans in Tabriz. Francis I of France, on the other hand, allied himself with the Turks to fight the German Emperor. The Ottoman Sultans, the Shahs of Persia, the Mughal Emperors all maintained active diplomatic exchanges with the western powers. Trade likewise crossed the frontiers constantly. The west required raw materials and luxury goods from the east; the east, similarly, needed raw materials and technical knowledge from the west. The Italian trading cities had long had footholds all over the Near East; later, they were joined by Spaniards, French, British and others. The discovery of the sea-route via the Cape of Good Hope gradually undermined the commanding position of the Near East in trade between Europe and Asia; Portuguese, French, British, Dutch and others all set up their trading stations in India and elsewhere in eastern waters.

Diplomats and merchants acquired a direct and intimate knowledge of the Oriental world, but a multitude of commercial, cultural and artistic exchanges brought some contact with the east even to those who did not travel. Mehmet II, the Ottoman conqueror of Constantinople, invited Gentile Bellini and other Italian artists to work for him. Carpaccio and other Venetian painters around 1500 filled their pictures with exotic figures in Oriental costumes. Though Europeans in general felt a certain horror for the ferocious Turks, they were none the less extremely interested in their customs, social organization, and particularly in their appearance and dress. European artists such as Pieter Coeck and Melchior Lorichs, who had travelled in Turkey, produced numerous prints of the people and places they had seen. The illustrated manuals of costume, popular in the 16th century, generally included plates of Oriental dress, and Turkish costumes exercised a certain influence on European fashions. In the field of textile design the influence was mutual. Italian silks and velvets were shipped to the east and influenced the designs of Oriental fabrics; at the same time eastern silks and velvets arrived in Europe and influenced designs there. In architecture and the fine arts it is more difficult to detect specific influences, but it was no mere coincidence that the great domed buildings of Europe were rising in the same centuries as the great domed buildings of the Islamic world. In the minor arts, Venice was the principal gateway for the arrival of Islamic ornament in Europe. Oriental craftsmen working there produced metalwork in a wholly eastern style. Pattern-books of arabesque or moresque ornament were published there from 1527 onwards and were promptly imitated in other publishing centres; in 1548 a pattern-book of this kind was issued in London. Indeed, in the second and third quarters of the 16th century arabesque or moresque ornament was the height of fashion and examples of it can be found in all the decorative arts of Europe. Imports of Oriental carpets should thus be regarded, not as an isolated phenomenon, but as one aspect of a general European receptiveness towards eastern ornament, albeit a very important aspect, since the carpets brought original Oriental designs directly into European homes.

We are singularly ill-informed about the organization of the carpet workshops and about the carpet trade. It is common sense to suppose that large, well designed and well executed carpets were produced in flourishing urban environments, whereas small and less refined pieces could have been produced by out-workers in villages. It is common sense to suppose that the finest carpets, and especially carpets with silk pile and gold thread, were produced in centres which enjoyed the patronage of royal courts. The export of carpets to Europe must have been of some commercial benefit to the workshops, particularly those in the Mediterranean area, but it is probable that the export trade took only a small proportion of total production. Virtually all Oriental carpets appear to be designed for local markets; apart from the inclusion of coats of arms for a special order, designs do not seem to have been modified to suit European clients. The merchants were evidently content to accept the stock designs and, indeed, East India Company documents suggest that bespoke carpets were apt to be both dearer and less well made than normal production. Although enormous numbers of Oriental carpets must have arrived in Europe during the period under consideration, it does not seem that the trade was sufficiently important to justify a high degree of organization. The documents concerning Cardinal Wolsey's collection of carpets show him acquiring them from friends and colleagues, as bribes from merchants, or as diplomatic gifts; there is no indication of any regular carpet dealers in London. A few English ships trading to the Levant in this period brought back Turkey carpets but not, apparently, in large numbers. A century later the East India Company was shipping Indian carpets and selling them at auction in London,

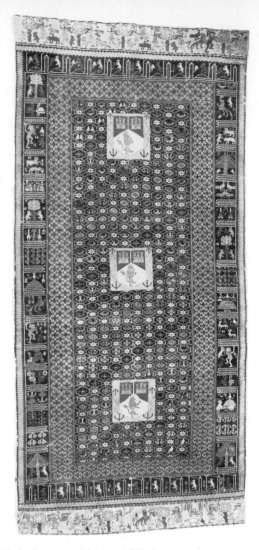

26 'Admiral' carpet with arms of Enriquez
Spain, second or third quarter 15th century
Philadelphia Museum of Art, no. 55.65.21;
The Joseph Lees Williams Memorial Collection,
Bequest of Mrs Mary A. Williams.

27 Pile carpet (detail), England, dated 1603
Victoria and Albert Museum, London, no. 710–1904.

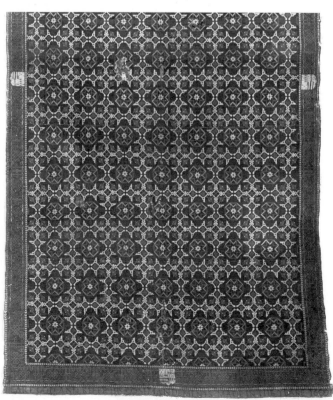

but the sales do not seem to have been a great commercial success and were discontinued. One has the impression that in London, at least, the carpet trade was a rather irregular and sporadic business; nevertheless the carpets continued to arrive. No doubt the trade was more active nearer the sources of supply, in Italy or in central Europe.

15th–16th century: the octagon style

The most popular textile designs of the Middle Ages, derived from ancient Sassanian and Byzantine models, were repeating patterns of circles containing animals or birds; in coarse woollen stuffs such as carpets, however, it was difficult to render circles satisfactorily and hence they were simplified into octagons. Designs of this type are seen in floor-coverings depicted in many Italian paintings from about 1300 onwards, but it is by no means certain that these were all Oriental pile carpets (fig. 3). No such doubts attach to two surviving 15th century rugs, clearly of Near Eastern origin, one of which comes from an unidentified church in central Italy (no. 1) and the other from the church of Marby in Sweden (no. 2). The Marby rug shows, within the octagons, a very stylized version of the ancient motif of a pair of birds confronted on either side of a tree. The other rug, also with octagons, has a wonderfully dynamic rendering of a Chinese dragon and phoenix, a motif which had been brought to the Near East by the Mongols; carpets with a similar pattern appear in 15th century Italian paintings (fig. 5).

Probably somewhat older than the two animal rugs is a remarkable Spanish carpet from a church in the Tyrol, with a design of a flowering tree which, once again, appears to derive from ancient Sassanian models (no. 3). Other Spanish carpets have diaper patterns of small octagons containing stars; these were often made to order, with coats of arms (fig. 26; no. 4).

The vast majority of carpets used in Europe during the second half of the 15th century and the first half of the 16th had geometrical patterns based on octagons; the patterns do, it is true, include a few elements derived from non-geometrical motifs such as foliage or script, but these are also treated in a highly geometrical fashion. Such geometrical patterns had long been important in Oriental carpets, but it seems as if the tremendous successes of the Ottoman Turks in the Near East heralded a new and more puritan era in carpet design, from which residual naturalistic elements such as animal and tree patterns were virtually eliminated. One of the most successful of the new generation of Anatolian designs, at least in terms of exports to Europe, was the so-called small Holbein pattern (nos. 6–11). This was a fairly small repeating pattern based on an alternation of octagonal and cross-shaped motifs, on a dark blue or green ground which suited the European preference for such colours in interior decoration (compare, for example, the taste for verdure tapestries and for table covers of green woollen cloth). Carpets of this type first appear in Italian painting in 1451 and are depicted quite frequently during the later 15th and 16th centuries (figs. 8, 15); they are still occasionally seen in 17th century paintings such as that of the *Somerset House Conference, 1604* (cover). Many thousands of small-pattern Holbein carpets must have been imported from Anatolia, but they were also produced in Spain (no. 7) and a version of the pattern appears in an English carpet dated 1603 (fig. 27). Such was the vogue of the small Holbein pattern that versions of it were also used for a number of table-carpets in needlework, made in various European countries between 1533 and the early 17th century.

Another very successful Anatolian design was the so-called large Holbein pattern, seen in carpets depicted in many European paintings of the later 15th and first half of the 16th century, and occasionally down to the early 17th century (front endpaper; figs. 7, 19, 28). This is a repeating pattern consisting of large octagons like those of the early animal carpets, but with stars, or motifs derived from script replacing the animals. These patterns, too, were copied by the Spanish carpet workshops (figs. 29, 30; no. 13) and versions of them appear in 16th century European needle-work carpets (fig. 31). Different but related patterns are seen in other classes of Anatolian rugs, such as the Memling and Crivelli patterns, named after rugs depicted by those painters (fig. 18; nos. 14, 15).

Designs of octagons far more ambitious than anything seen in Anatolian rugs were produced in the Cairo workshops for the so-called Mamluk carpets, which were first made in the late 15th century under the Mamluk dynasty, but continued in production under the Ottomans at least until the middle of the 16th century if not later (nos. 17–25). The superb, newly discovered Mamluk carpet from the Pitti Palace, the largest of its kind, entered the Medici collection

28 Large-pattern Holbein carpet
　Turkey, second half 15th century
　Philadelphia Museum of Art, no. 43.40.67;
　McIlhenny Collection, Bequest of John D. McIlhenny.

29 Large-pattern Holbein carpet
　Spain, possibly Alcaraz, second half 15th century
　The Saint Louis Art Museum, no. 122.1929.

as late as 1557–71 (no. 21). Very large Mamluk carpets such as this one generally have three huge octagons in the length of the field, each one with a complex satellite system of smaller octagons and other geometrical forms ranged about it; smaller pieces generally have just one large octagon surrounded by an arrangement of smaller forms (nos. 22, 23). Related designs are seen in the so-called para-Mamluk rugs and compartment rugs, made in Turkey by workshops which were probably founded by weavers from Cairo (nos. 28–30).

One further Anatolian design, the so-called Lotto pattern, was also based on octagons (nos. 31–5). It is in some respects a revised version of the small Holbein pattern, in which the severely geometrical shapes of the original are softened into tendrils and leaf-like forms. Lotto rugs were exported to Europe in enormous numbers over a very long period; they first appear in an Italian painting of 1516 and are still common in Dutch paintings of the third quarter of the 17th century (figs. 11, 21, 23). Besides those from Anatolia, Lotto rugs were also produced in Spain and in England (no. 33).

30 Carpet with stars in octagons
Spain, possibly Alcaraz, middle or second half
15th century
The Textile Museum, Washington, D.C., no. R44.00.5.

Near Eastern rugs with octagon patterns, all originally
designed in the 15th or early 16th centuries, may well have
owed a good deal to the influence of Persian designs. But
few, if any, Persian carpets reached Europe at that early
period and our knowledge of them is based mainly on representations in Persian miniatures. One north-west Persian
carpet in the exhibition, however, from the Museum of Fine
Arts in Boston, has a repeating pattern distantly related to
the small Holbein pattern and gives at least some indication
of the character of Persian designs of this type (no. 57).

16th century: the medallion style

Near Eastern carpets with octagon patterns continued in
production, as we have seen, for most of the 16th century
and even, particularly in the case of small Lotto rugs, down
to the second half of the 17th century. The Turkish carpet
industry obviously aimed at large scale production for a
mass market and continued weaving the same field patterns
for as long as they would sell, varying only the border patterns in line with current fashions. The Cairene workshops
aimed at a higher level of the market and produced very
varied designs, though always within the same stylistic repertory. Despite the persistence of these old octagon designs,
however, a new generation of carpet designs of a very different character came to the fore in the Near East in the second
and third quarters of the 16th century. These designs were
not geometrical, but free, flowing and floral. They were unquestionably inspired by Persian carpets.

31 Needlework carpet
England (?), 16th century
Victoria and Albert Museum, London, no. T.41–1928.

In so far as we are able to judge it, Persian carpet production of the 16th century, under the Safavid dynasty, was aimed at various levels of the market, but mostly towards the upper end. It is of course possible that our picture of it may be somewhat distorted by the fact that only the better carpets were valuable enough to be worth exporting, or worth preserving inside Persia, while inferior grades have disappeared. At all events it is quite clear that the Persian industry produced numbers of carpets of luxurious quality and that many of them were specially designed by highly skilled artists. Some of these artists may have been miniature painters, for the details of the designs are very like those found in manuscripts, while the layout of the carpets, generally with a large medallion in the centre and sometimes with quarter-medallions in the corners, owes something to the designs of book-bindings.

A group of medallion carpets from north-west Persia, an area which was repeatedly occupied by the Ottoman Turks during the first half of the 16th century, show a few Turkish details in the design, but are otherwise thoroughly Persian (nos. 58–60). They have superb central medallions, superimposed on very large repeating patterns of coiling stems, within handsome arabesque borders. Strong and wonderfully satisfying though these designs are, they can hardly emulate the best of the artist-designed medallion carpets, such as the Ardabil carpet of 1539/40 in the Victoria and Albert Museum, London (fig. 32), or the somewhat later Anhalt carpet in the Metropolitan Museum of Art, New York (no. 62). Note that in carpets of the highest quality such as these, the coiling stems are not simply an underlying repeating pattern, as in the north-west Persian group just mentioned, but are freely drawn and are integrated, together with the great medallions and their satellite cartouches, into a single grand design. Another superb 16th century Persian medallion carpet which is always on view in London is the so-called Chelsea carpet in the Victoria and Albert Museum; it differs from the more usual designs in having several medallions, and the field pattern, instead of coiling stems, shows birds and animals among trees (fig. 33). Yet another demonstration of the versatility of the Persian carpet designers is the wonderful carpet from Lyon, with its splendid pattern of many small medallions with radiating cartouches (no. 61). These are unquestionably some of the greatest carpets in the world.

Besides the superb medallion carpets with woollen pile, workshops thought to have been located at Kashan also produced still more luxurious carpets, very finely knotted in silk pile, supplemented by gold and silver thread. These carpets, the height of the carpet weavers' art, were obviously produced for court patrons. Three exquisite large carpets of this class have survived, one from the former Imperial Collection in Vienna, one in Boston from the Torrigiani Collection, and one, which we are privileged to include in this exhibition, in the Royal Collections in Stockholm (no. 65). All three are specially designed pieces, with central and corner medallions, and field patterns of men hunting wild animals among coiling floral stems. A dozen or two smaller silk carpets of comparable quality have survived. Most of them have medallion designs, with coiling floral stems in the field (nos. 67, 68). A few have designs of animals in a landscape (no. 66). A further group of silk-and-gold pieces are not pile carpets, but are flat-woven in the tapestry technique; they generally have medallion or cartouche designs (nos. 71, 72). One example shown here, with the

32 The Ardabil Carpet
Persia, 1539/40
Victoria and Albert Museum, London, no. 272–1893.

arms of the King of Poland, is known to have been woven at Kashan in 1601–2 (no. 73).

It is difficult to estimate how many Persian carpets reached Europe in the 16th century, but certainly by the second half of the century they began to be recorded in some numbers in the inventories of the European nobility. No doubt by that time they were being shipped by the sea-route round the Cape of Good Hope as well as by land-routes to the Black Sea or Mediterranean ports. An interesting testimony to English interest in Persian carpets are the instructions given by Richard Hakluyt to 'Morgan Hubblethorne, Dier, sent into Persia, 1579'; Hubblethorne was to make a special study of Persian techniques of dyeing woollen yarn for carpets and, if possible, to bring back a Persian carpet weaver to England.

Persian carpets certainly remained articles of high luxury for Europe at this time, but for clients who wished to achieve similar effects at lower cost the so-called Star Ushak and

33 The Chelsea Carpet
   Persia, second quarter 16th century
   Victoria and Albert Museum, London, no. 589–1890.

Medallion Ushak carpets made in Turkish workshops were
an excellent substitute (nos. 36, 38–41). Star Ushak carpets
appear in European paintings from 1534 onwards and the
grander Medallion Ushak carpets from about 1570 onwards.
These are fine, original designs and thoroughly Turkish in
many respects, but they were inspired by Persian examples
and can be considered, in some sense, as commercial versions
of the great artist-designed Persian carpets like the Ardabil
and Chelsea carpets. They are large repeating patterns fea-
turing medallions and cartouches of various shapes and sizes,
often containing arabesque ornament, on field patterns of
floral stems. Following the usual practice of the Turkish
workshops, these designs, once established, were repeated
for generations and indeed the Medallion Ushak design,
in modified forms, persisted until modern times. Besides
Turkish examples, the exhibition includes a Star Ushak
carpet made in England in 1585 (no. 37) and a Medallion
Ushak carpet made in Poland in the 17th century (no. 42).
Another group of Turkish carpets which were exported to

Europe and sometimes copied there were the white-ground
carpets, produced in the later 16th and early 17th centuries
(nos. 43–5).

The Cairo workshops continued to supply Europe with
large numbers of carpets, mainly up-market products with a
considerable variety of designs, but all based on the same repertory of ornament. About the middle years of the 16th century there was a quite abrupt switch from the older repertory
of octagon designs to a new style of floral stems and feathery
leaves, inspired in a general way by Persian carpets, but
based more specifically on the ornament of Turkish tiles.
Many examples had medallions in the Persian manner (nos.
50–3). Others, including a huge, newly discovered carpet
from the Pitti Palace, which entered the Medici collection
in 1623, have repeating patterns of floral motifs without
medallions (nos. 49, 56).

Somewhat surprisingly, prayer rugs from the Near East,
originally intended for Muslim prayer, were imported quite
extensively into Europe (figs. 9, 10, 34; nos. 16, 19, 46–8,
54, 55). In England they were rather charmingly called
muskitto or muskets carpets, i.e. mosque carpets.

34 Coupled-column prayer rug
   Turkey, 17th century
   The Textile Museum, Washington, D.C.,
   no. R34.22.1.

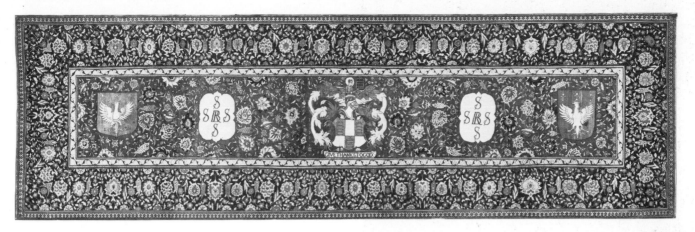

35 The Girdlers' Carpet
India, Mughal empire, 1631–2
The Worshipful Company of Girdlers, London.

17th century: the floral style

Though designs with medallions were the height of fashion in the 16th century, the medallions were not regarded as indispensable even at that period, and they became progressively less important in carpet designs of the 17th century. All-over designs of coiling stems with flowers and large palmettes, sometimes with animals, were favoured in various Persian carpet weaving centres from the later 16th century onwards and have been particularly associated with Herat in eastern Persia (no. 74). Other related carpets were woven in the workshops set up by the Mughal emperors in northern India, initially staffed by Persian weavers; the exhibition includes two outstanding Mughal animal carpets of this class, one from the Museum of Islamic Art in Berlin and the other from an English private collection (nos. 76, 77). Very large numbers of carpets of this type, but generally without animals, were exported from Persia and India to Europe and are seen in innumerable European paintings of the 17th century (fig. 24; no. 75). It was also possible to order carpets with coats of arms from the workshops in India and two notable examples are still preserved in London, namely the Girdlers' Carpet at Girdlers' Hall, woven for Robert Bell in Lahore 1631–2, and the Fremlin carpet at the Victoria and Albert Museum, woven for William Fremlin about 1640; the former has a floral pattern (fig. 35; and see Irwin, 1962), the latter a pattern of animals in a landscape (fig. 36). Remarkably, it was also possible, about the same period, to order British-made copies of Indian floral carpets; an example discovered only two or three years ago at Glamis Castle, now at the National Museum of Antiquities, Edinburgh, includes the monogram of John Lyon, second Earl of Kinghorne, and his wife, but it is not certain whether the reference is to his first marriage in 1618, or his second marriage about 1640 (fig. 37; and see *Hali*, 11, no. 4, 1980, pp. 346–7).

A group of Persian floral carpets which were extensively imported into Europe were the silk-pile carpets made at Isfahan and elsewhere. With their original brilliant colours, now too often dulled, and the glitter of their gold and silver thread, they made a marvellous complement to the decor and furniture of Baroque palaces and mansions. The exhibition includes the large example with unidentified coats of arms, formerly in the Czartoryski Collection, now in the Metropolitan Museum of Art, which gave them their misleading title of 'Polonaise' or Polish carpets (no. 69).

36 The Fremlin carpet showing coats of arms (detail)
India, Mughal empire, *c.* 1640
Victoria and Albert Museum, London, no. IM1–1936.

Another group of Persian carpets with beautiful floral designs are the so-called vase carpets, believed to have been made in the Kerman area. Examples selected for the exhibition include a fragment of one of the earliest and finest carpets of this type and a later piece formerly in a church in Poland (nos. 78, 79). Also present is a superb small rug related to the vase carpets, the so-called Corcoran throne rug, with a striking design of sickle-shaped leaves (no. 80). The vase design exercised some influence in Mughal India and was the inspiration of a Mughal palace carpet shown here, notable for its gigantic size (no. 81).

A further group of floral designs found in Mughal Indian carpets show more or less naturalistic flowering plants, on plain backgrounds or within some kind of trellis (nos. 82–4). These designs, inspired in part by European botanical illustrations, were originally devised for the Indian workshops,

38 'Portuguese' carpet (detail)
Persia or India, middle 17th century
The National Trust, Knole.

37 The Strathmore Carpet
England, first half 17th century
National Museum of Antiquities of Scotland, Edinburgh.

but were later imitated in Persia (no. 86). Among the Indian examples is a well-known, beautifully designed and very finely executed prayer rug, from the Thyssen-Bornemisza Collection (no. 85).

Finally, one other small group of carpets may be briefly mentioned. These are the so-called Portuguese carpets, which are of some interest since they show, in the corners of an otherwise floral design, a scene of sailing vessels with European mariners – the only appearance of European figures in the designs of early Oriental carpets. They have been attributed both to Persia and to India (see Ellis, 1975). The Portuguese carpets are not represented in the exhibition, but an example can be seen not far from London, at Knole, in Kent (fig. 38).

Acknowledgements will be found elsewhere in this catalogue, but I may perhaps conclude with a few personal words of thanks. First of all I am deeply indebted to the Arts Council of Great Britain for inviting me to undertake the delightful task of selecting carpets for this exhibition. Secondly, I would like to thank the devoted staff of the Arts Council, Joanna Drew, Andrew Dempsey, Susan Ferleger Brades, Norman McManus, Jocelyn Poulton and others, who have worked tirelessly to turn this project into reality. David Sylvester, has been a wonderfully inspiring collaborator, while Michael Franses has contributed an irrepressible flow of valuable ideas on all aspects of the show. I owe thanks to the curators of many collections around the world, too numerous to be named here individually, who have received me with the greatest kindness and courtesy and who, when presented with difficult requests for loans at very short notice, have very rarely refused them. I am grateful to May Beattie for helpful advice and for allowing her essay to be reprinted in this catalogue. I offer my sincerest thanks to Mr. and Mrs. Charles Grant Ellis, who received me in their home for an entire weekend during the preparation of the exhibition and wonderfully instructed and entertained me, with carpet-lore and carpet-anecdote. My one regret concerning the otherwise entirely pleasurable enterprise of this exhibition is that I have had too little time to prepare a catalogue which would do full justice to the quality of the exhibits. But I hope that the catalogue entries, together with the bibliography (which makes no claim to be comprehensive), will at least serve to direct the reader to sources of further information if he so desires.

3 Flowering tree carpet, sometimes called the Synagogue carpet
  (detail)
  Southern Spain, 14th century
  Staatliche Museen zu Berlin, Islamisches Museum.
  (Not in exhibition)

2 Animal rug, known as the Marby rug
Anatolia, first half or middle 15th century
Stockholm, Statens Historiska Museum.

1 Animal rug, known as the dragon-and-phoenix rug
Anatolia, first half or middle 15th century
Staatliche Museen zu Berlin, Islamisches Museum.
(Not in exhibition)

34

15 Crivelli rug, fragment
Anatolia, second half 15th century or later
Budapest, Museum of Applied Arts
(Iparmüvészeti Muzeum).

14 Rug with Memling motif, fragments
Anatolia, second half 15th century or later
Budapest, Museum of Applied Arts
(Iparmüvészeti Muzeum).

7 Small-pattern Holbein carpet
Southern Spain, second half 15th century
Boston, Museum of Fine Arts; Elizabeth H. Flint Fund in
memory of Sarah Gore Flint Townsend.

5 Silk-pattern carpet
Southern Spain, second half 15th century
Washington, D.C., The Textile Museum.

44 White ground bird carpet
Anatolia, late 16th or early 17th century
Wher Collection, Switzerland.

34 Lotto rug
Anatolia or south-eastern Europe,
late 16th or first half 17th century
Budapest, Museum of Applied Arts
(Iparmüvészeti Muzeum).

16 Prayer rug of Bellini type
Anatolia, late 15th or early 16th century
Berlin, Staatliche Museen Preussischer Kulturbesitz,
Museum für Islamische Kunst.

41 Medallion Ushak carpet
Anatolia, 16th or early 17th century
Lugano, Switzerland, Thyssen–Bornemisza Collection.

23 Mamluk carpet
   Egypt, Cairo, first half or middle 16th century
   Boston, Museum of Fine Arts; Harriet Otis Cruft Fund.

21 The Medici Mamluk carpet
Egypt, Cairo, first half or middle 16th century
Florence, Palazzo Pitti.

56 The Medici Ottoman carpet
Egypt, Cairo, early 17th century
Florence, Palazzo Pitti.

41

58 Medallion carpet
North-west Persia, 16th century
Lisbon, Calouste Gulbenkian Museum.

65 The Swedish Royal hunting carpet
Persia, possibly Kashan, late 16th century
Stockholm, The Royal Collections.

73 Silk tapestry rug
Persia, Kashan, 1601–2
Munich, Bayerische Verwaltung der Staatlichen Schlösser,
Gärten und Seen, Residenzmuseum.

78 Vase carpet, fragment
Persia, possibly Kerman, early 17th century
Berlin, Staatliche Museen Preussischer Kulturbesitz,
Museum für Islamische Kunst.

80 Sickle-leaf rug
   Persia, possibly Kerman, first half 17th century
   Washington, D.C., The Corcoran Gallery of Art; Bequest of
   William A. Clark, 1926.

85 Prayer rug, incomplete
India, Mughal empire, second quarter or middle 17th century
Lugano, Switzerland, Thyssen–Bornemisza Collection.

81 Carpet with vase design (detail)
India, Mughal empire, 17th century
John Hewett Collection.

Catalogue of the Exhibition

TURKISH, EGYPTIAN AND EUROPEAN CARPETS

Animal carpets

Animal motifs have appeared in carpet patterns since ancient times; a carpet of about the 5th–3rd century BC found at Pazyryk in the Altai Mountains includes figures of deer, horses and winged monsters. In the Middle Ages patterns of circles containing birds and animals were universally employed in the textile arts, but in carpets the circles were generally rendered as octagons.

Many floor-carpets with patterns of animals and birds are depicted in Italian paintings of the 14th and 15th centuries (figs. 3, 5) and some also in Spanish and Persian paintings. Most of those in the Italian paintings lack the characteristic borders of Near Eastern rugs and it has been tentatively suggested that they may have been made in Italy. But the rare carpets and fragments with animals and birds which have been found in Turkey and Egypt are evidently of Near Eastern manufacture and the same is true of the two examples which have been found in Europe, one from a church in Italy (no. 1), the other from a church in Sweden (no. 2).

During the 15th century, by a remarkable revolution of taste, the patterns of animals and birds, which had dominated the textile arts for centuries, fell from general favour and non-representational or plant motifs came to be preferred, in carpets as in other textiles.

Literature
Ettinghausen, 1959; Durul & Aslanapa; Mills, 1978.

I

1 **Animal rug, known as the dragon-and-phoenix rug**

Anatolia, first half or middle 15th century
L. 172 cm. W. 90 cm.
Staatliche Museen zu Berlin, Islamisches Museum,
no. I.4
(Not in exhibition)
REPRODUCED IN COLOUR PAGE 34

Said to have come from a church in central Italy, this extraordinary rug was acquired by Wilhelm von Bode in Rome in 1886. The superbly stylized design in the octagons represents the combat of the phoenix and the dragon, ancient Chinese motifs which had been transmitted to the Islamic world by the Mongols. Good evidence for the date of the rug is provided by Italian paintings. The same pattern, similarly stylized and in similar colouring of red and blue on a white or yellow ground, is seen in a large floor-carpet depicted by the Sienese painter Domenico di Bartolo in 1440 and in small rugs depicted by the Modenese painter Bartolommeo degli Erri in the 1470s (fig. 5). A fragment of carpet with the same pattern, again in similar colouring, has been found at Fostat in Egypt. These pieces are generally attributed to Anatolia, though the Caucasus has also been suggested as a possible origin. The border pattern of S-shapes is found in a number of early Turkish and other carpets. A recent suggestion (*Hali*, IV, no. 1, 1981, p. 31) that the markings on the body of the topmost phoenix are an Armenian inscription seems fanciful. The numerous differences between the combat scenes in the two octagons show that the weaver interpreted the motif with remarkable freedom of hand.

Literature
Sarre & Trenkwald, 1929, pl. 1; Erdmann, 1955; Mills, 1978, pp. 236–7, 242.

2 Animal rug, known as the Marby rug

Anatolia, first half or middle 15th century
L. 145 cm. W. 109 cm.
Stockholm, Statens Historiska Museum, no. 17 786
REPRODUCED IN COLOUR PAGE 34

This boldly designed rug was formerly in the church at
Marby, Jämtland, Sweden. Patterns of circles containing
two birds standing symmetrically on either side of a tree
were very common in woven silks and woollens from the
early Middle Ages onwards. Floor-carpets showing the
birds and tree in octagons instead of circles were depicted
by a number of Sienese painters between 1317 and the
1470s, but they do not correspond very closely with the
treatment of the motif seen in the Marby rug. Between the
Marby rug and the Berlin dragon-and-phoenix rug,
however, there are close relationships in stylization, in
colouring and in technical details – notably the lines of
knots at intervals on the back of the rugs. The two rugs
are generally assumed to be of similar date and origin. The
patterns of the border and guard stripes are
characteristically Anatolian; the same guard stripes appear
in one of the group of early carpets found in the mosque
of Ala-ad-din at Konya and in other early Turkish rugs.
The web ends and selvages are remarkably preserved for a
rug of this age.

Literature
Sarre & Trenkwald, 1929, pl. 2; Lamm, 1937, p. 104 ff.

2

Early Spanish carpets

For much of the Middle Ages southern Spain was a powerful
Muslim state, with a distinguished record in learning and
the arts. There is some evidence that carpets were produced
and exported from the province of Murcia from the 12th
century onwards and after the Christian reconquest carpet
production continued in this area, for a time, no doubt,
employing Muslim workers. Spanish carpets are said to
have been brought to London in 1255 for the marriage of
Eleanor of Castile and the future Edward I and they are also
recorded in French documents of the 14th and 15th centuries.
Surviving Spanish carpets from this period differ from those
of the Near East not only in the details of their designs, but
also in their characteristic knotting technique, with the pile
threads wrapped around a single warp end instead of two as
was usual in the Near East. Fragments of early Spanish
carpets have been found in Egypt and a complete carpet in
the Berlin collection, possibly of 14th century date, was
formerly in a church in the Tyrol (no. 3).

A group of large carpets, formerly in convents in Spain
and now nearly all in museums in the United States, show
Spanish coats of arms on a field pattern composed of a
diaper of small octagonal compartments containing stars
and other motifs in alternation (fig. 26; no. 4). These carpets
are of 15th century date, but the type goes back to the 14th
century. Pope John XXII (reigned 1316–34) is known to
have acquired Spanish armorial carpets for the papal palace
at Avignon and a wall-painting in the palace, datable 1344–6,
depicts a carpet with the characteristic field pattern of small
octagons and stars (fig. 2). Another type of Spanish carpet
has a pattern derived from 15th century silks and velvets
(no. 5). Others have patterns of the small Holbein and large
Holbein types, imitated from Turkish carpets (nos. 7, 13).
The towns of Letur and Alcaraz in Murcia are mentioned as
centres of carpet production in the 15th century.

Literature
Ferrandis Torres, 1933; May, 1945; Dimand, 1973, p. 251 ff.; Mackie, 1977
and 1979.

3 Flowering tree carpet, sometimes called the Synagogue carpet

Southern Spain, 14th century
L. 303 cm. W. 94 cm.
Staatliche Museen zu Berlin, Islamisches Museum, no. I.27
(Not in exhibition)
REPRODUCED IN COLOUR PAGE 33

This carpet was acquired in 1880 from a church in the
Tyrol. The unique design appears to represent a highly
stylized tree or plant with huge tulip-like blossoms, a motif
formulated in the sculpture and metalwork of Sassanian
Persia and continued in the textile arts of the early Islamic
period, for example in a famous central Asian silk textile
preserved at Nancy. The motif also appears in the Islamic
and Mudejar art of Spain, as in the fine stucco reliefs of
about 1355 in the synagogue of the Tránsito at Toledo.
This carpet presents the motif in a rectilinear version in
which the blossoms, while retaining their original shape,
have been embellished with what appear to be architectural
elements such as doors and roofs. Friedrich Sarre suggested
that they represent the Jewish Ark of the Law. Lack of
any closely comparable material makes it difficult to date

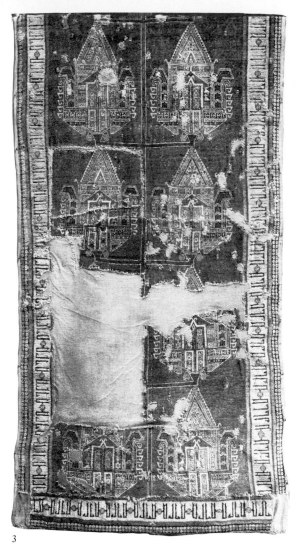

3

the carpet, but the uniqueness of its design and the simplicity of the Kufic border, based on the name of Allah, suggest a date earlier than that of the 15th century Spanish armorial carpets.

Literature
Sarre, 1930.

4 Armorial carpet

incomplete

Southern Spain, first half or middle 15th century
L. 397 cm. W. 224 cm.
Washington, D.C., The Textile Museum, no. R44.4.1

This is one of a set of three matching carpets said to have come from the convent of Santa Isabel de los Reyes, Toledo; the other two belong to the Hispanic Society of America and the Detroit Institute of Arts. The field pattern, a network of small octagonal compartments containing alternately six-pointed stars and other motifs (stylized birds, human figures, etc.) resembles the pattern of a carpet depicted in a wall-painting of 1344–6 by Matteo di Giovanetti in the Palace of the Popes at Avignon (fig. 2). The heraldic shields arranged at intervals over the field display the arms of Aragon impaling Castile-Leon, presumably relating to the marriage in 1415 of Alfonso of Aragon and Maria of Castile; both died in 1458. These carpets with the arms of Aragon and Castile and another series with the arms of the Enriquez family from the convent of Santa Clara at Palencia (fig. 26), have been

tentatively attributed to Letur. Armorial carpets were evidently a speciality of the Spanish workshops; the inventory of Martin I of Aragon, 1410, has two such carpets, while that of the Duc de Berry, 1416, includes a Spanish carpet with the arms of Cardinal de Viviers and another with the arms of Castile.

Carpets of similar format, having narrow fields with small diaper patterns surrounded with an imposing array of borders and guard stripes, were current in Anatolia from the 13th century onwards, for example, the carpets found in the mosques of Konya and Beyshehir. The Spanish carpets may have been inspired by these Turkish models, but the details of their fields and borders seem characteristically Spanish. The outer border of spiky pseudo-Kufic script is unfortunately mutilated and incomplete in this example. Holbein, in his *Solothurn Madonna* of 1522, depicts a Spanish armorial carpet with just such borders; the arms are those of Johann Gerster, town clerk of Basle, and his wife. Did this couple commission a carpet from Spain, or did Holbein substitute their arms for those which actually existed on the carpet he copied?

Literature
Van de Put, 1911; Kühnel & Bellinger, 1953, pp. 9–10, pls. IV–VIII; Mackie, 1977, pp. 21–2.

4

5 Silk-pattern carpet

Southern Spain, second half 15th century
L. 234 cm. W. 165 cm.
Washington, D.C., The Textile Museum, no. R44.2.1
REPRODUCED IN COLOUR PAGE 36

This is a fine example of a group of Spanish carpets
(others are in museums in London, Madrid, New York
and Washington, D.C.) with a field pattern derived from
the so-called pomegranate or lobed-leaf design, which
dominated 15th century silk-weaving in Italy and, to a
lesser extent, in Spain and the Near East. The silk
prototype of this particular design, having parts of the
pattern hatched with short horizontal lines, dates from the
second half of the 15th century. Some Turkish rugs also
have patterns based on silk designs of comparable type
(e.g. Erdmann, 1970, fig. 117, reproduced upside down),
but it is not clear whether there was any direct influence
between these and the Spanish examples. The borders and
end bands of the present carpet are stiffer and presumably
later versions of those of the armorial carpets (fig. 26;
no. 4); the uprights of the old pseudo-Kufic pattern
remain, but have lost any resemblance to script. The
carpet has been attributed to Alcaraz.

Literature
Kühnel & Bellinger, 1953, p. 19, pls. XVIII, XIX; Mackie, 1979, p. 90.

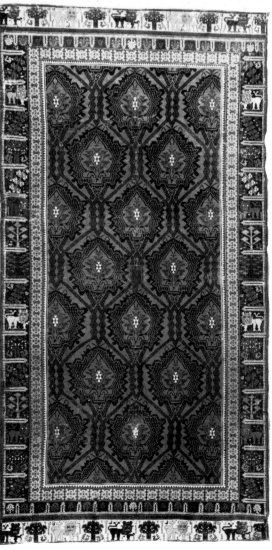

5

Small-pattern Holbein carpets

Hans Holbein the Younger painted various Turkish carpets
with patterns of octagons, including one with small octagons
which appears in a portrait painted in London in 1532 and
others with large octagons which appear in various pictures,
mostly painted in London between 1527 and 1543. The two
types are generally called small-pattern and large-pattern
Holbein carpets (or sometimes Holbein type I and Holbein
type III), clumsy terms which are also rather misleading,
since both types were depicted by painters long before
Holbein was born. The small Holbein pattern is a repeating
pattern composed of two main elements, an octagon with an
outline of angular interlace and a cross-shaped motif of
arabesque forms. It is also possible to read the pattern as one
of octagons in square compartments with arabesque forms
filling the corners of the squares; this aspect was sometimes
made apparent by alternating the colours of the squares, like
a chessboard (no. 9). The basic layout of more or less circular
motifs with more or less cross-shaped motifs between them
is an ancient one, which was very widespread in the textile
arts of the Middle Ages. A carpet with a pattern somewhat
akin to that of the small-pattern Holbein carpets is seen in a
Persian miniature as early as 1429/30, but as far as we know
the small Holbein pattern itself was formulated in Anatolia.
It was enormously successful. Paintings indicate that carpets
of this type were exported to western Europe in large
numbers and were widely used as floor-carpets and table-
carpets. Their first appearance is in a wall-painting of 1451,
by Piero della Francesca. From then onwards they figure in
many Italian paintings, and subsequently in Spanish and
northern European paintings, down to about 1550 (figs. 8, 15).
Thereafter they appear only rarely, but they certainly remained in use (and possibly also in production) down to the
17th century; one of them was handsomely portrayed in *The
Somerset House Conference, 1604* (cover). The paintings provide useful evidence for the chronology of the various types
of pseudo-Kufic and interlace borders which are found on
most of the extant carpets of this type (nos. 6–10). No doubt
most of these carpets were produced in Anatolia, but they
were certainly copied in Spain (no. 7) and Charles Grant
Ellis has suggested that some may have been produced in
Italy and in south-eastern Europe (nos. 10, 11). Carpets
with variants of the small Holbein pattern were made in
Anatolia (no. 12), in Spain and in England (one dated 1603,
fig. 27). Needlework carpets with the small Holbein pattern
or variants of it were made in Switzerland, France, England
and Spain from 1533 to the early 17th century.

Literature
Erdmann, 1970, pp. 51–6; Mills, 1978; Pinner & Stanger, 1978.

6 Small-pattern Holbein carpet

fragment

Anatolia, second half 15th century
L. 94 cm. W. 193 cm.
The Keir Collection

Formerly in the Palazzo Salvadore, Florence, this is a
battered and patched remnant of a small-pattern Holbein
carpet of outstanding quality and unusually large format –

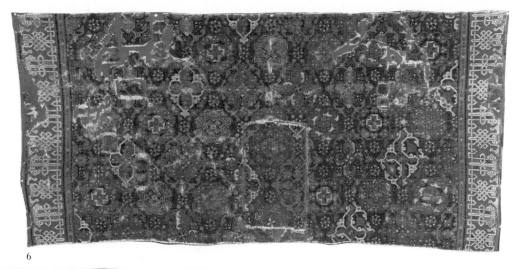

6

7

with seven octagons in the width and originally, no doubt, several metres long. The border, with long-stemmed pseudo-Kufic and interlace, is similar to the borders of small-pattern Holbein carpets in Mantegna's Verona altarpiece of 1459, in a miniature of about 1475 by Francesco di Giorgio, and in a Lucchese painting of the late 15th century; in all these, as in the present fragment, the border is red and the field blue-green. There is no reason to doubt that this fragment and another with a similar border in the Berlin collection were made in the time-bracket indicated by the paintings. Small-pattern Holbein carpets were often enlivened by alternation of colours in adjacent motifs, but in this piece the variation in the colours of the motifs has been carried to most unusual lengths, with colour schemes repeating in diagonal lines running from lower left to upper right, but not apparently, in the horizontal rows.

Literature
Spuhler, 1978, pp. 34–5, no. 5.

7   Small-pattern Holbein carpet

Southern Spain, second half 15th century
L. 463 cm. W. 206 cm.
Boston, Museum of Fine Arts, no. 39.614;
Elizabeth H. Flint Fund, in memory of
Sarah Gore Flint Townsend
REPRODUCED IN COLOUR PAGE 36

This superb carpet, knotted with the Spanish single-warp knot and with guard stripes in Spanish designs, is a Spanish copy of the earliest type of Turkish small-pattern Holbein carpets, with a pseudo-Kufic border of the type seen in no. 6 and in Italian paintings of the second half of the 15th century. It is interesting to note, however, that the border, which in the Turkish prototypes was designed to be 'read' by someone seated in the field of the carpet, is here reversed to conform to the usual Spanish practice, seen also in nos. 3 and 4 and fig. 26, of making such borders face outwards, except for the border at the top of the carpet. On the dark green field there are two basic colour schemes for each of the two main motifs, producing a well-marked diagonal and lattice effect.

Literature
Denny, 1978, p. 156; Mackie, 1979, p. 93.

8

carpet appear together in a carpet depicted in 1466–8 by the Florentine painter Filippo Lippi in Spoleto. There can be little doubt that the present carpet and a fragment of another small-pattern Holbein carpet with the same borders in the Türk ve Islâm Museum in Istanbul are of the same period as the paintings. On blue-green fields, both these carpets have two basic colour schemes for each of the two main motifs, producing diagonal and lattice effects.

Literature
Hali, 1, no. 4, 1978, colour plate III.

9 Small-pattern Holbein carpet

fragments

Anatolia, first half 16th century
L. 97 cm. W. 104 cm.
London, Victoria and Albert Museum, no. 154–1908

These fragments are exhibited as a token representation of a characteristic treatment of the field in small-pattern Holbein carpets, where the ground is divided up into red and blue-green squares and the cross-motifs have quartered colours, thus producing a chessboard effect. Similar effects are seen in carpets in Persian miniatures of the 15th century. Small-pattern Holbein carpets with this effect have been noted in Italian paintings of the 1520s and 1530s. Surviving examples in Berlin, the Keir Collection and elsewhere have border patterns similar to that seen in no. 10. These fragments, like other extant examples of small-pattern Holbein rugs with chessboard fields, were acquired in Italy.

Unpublished.

9

8 Small-pattern Holbein carpet

Anatolia, second half 15th century
L. 264 cm. W. 155 cm.
Wher Collection, Switzerland

Formerly in the Piero Barbieri Collection, Genoa, this remarkable piece appears at first sight to be virtually intact; in fact, both ends, with their borders, and both side edges are excellent modern reconstructions and there are careful repairs throughout. Nevertheless, this is still an outstanding carpet. Small-pattern Holbein carpets with the same rather rare type of pseudo-Kufic border are depicted by the Florentine painter Lorenzo di Credi in his Pistoia altarpiece of 1478–85 and by an unidentified painter in a late 15th century picture in the Duomo, Florence. The same border appears on other Turkish carpets depicted by the Florentine Domenico Ghirlandaio in 1480 and a little later. John Mills has noted that both the borders on the present

10

10 Small-pattern Holbein rug

Anatolia or south-eastern Europe, 16th century
L. 198 cm. W. 122 cm.
The Saint Louis Art Museum, no. 106:1929; gift of James
F. Ballard

Formerly in the collection of James F. Ballard and before
that with Kennedy in Berlin, this piece belongs to a group
of small-pattern Holbein rugs with red grounds, with
uniform colour schemes for each of the two main motifs,
and with interlace borders also on a red ground. Other
examples are in museums in Budapest, Munich,
Washington, D.C. and elsewhere. Variants of the border
pattern seen here appear in paintings from the 1490s, but
this particular form appears from the 1520s onwards; it is
also recorded in 1604 (cover). Compared with earlier
small-pattern Holbein carpets this group of small red rugs,
which are generally assigned to the 16th or early 17th
century, seem to represent a degree of simplification and
tiredness, or perhaps they were simply aimed at a more
modest market. Curiously, no small-pattern Holbein rugs
with red grounds have been noted in paintings; western
Europe evidently preferred the blue-green type. Were the
red-ground rugs exported from Anatolia to eastern rather
than western Europe? Or could they have been produced
in the European territories of the Ottoman Empire?

Literature
Dimand, 1935, pl. XIV.

11 Small-pattern Holbein rug

Anatolia or south-eastern Europe, 16th century
L. 220 cm. W. 154 cm.
Budapest, Museum of Applied Arts (Iparmüvészeti
Muzeum), no. 14785

This small rug with a dark green-blue ground has cross-
motifs with two alternating colour schemes and octagons
with quartered colours; the white-ground border has a
pattern of stars. The quartered octagons are rarely depicted
in western European paintings, though they are seen in
portraits produced in England, for example Flicke's
portrait of Archbishop Cranmer, 1546, and a portrait of
the young King Edward VI, *c.*1550, both in the National
Portrait Gallery, London (fig. 15). As with the Saint Louis
rug (no. 10) the question arises whether this may be a type
of rug exported from Anatolia mainly to eastern Europe,
or perhaps produced in the European territories of the
Ottoman Empire. Charles Grant Ellis has argued (orally)
for an eastern European origin. The long web ends and
wide selvages recall the Marby rug (no. 2) which also has
similar patterns in the guard stripes.

Literature
Batári, 1974, no. 1; Batári 1982, no. 4.

11

12

12 Variant small-pattern Holbein carpet

fragments used to cover an Italian Renaissance armchair

Anatolia, second half 15th century
Munich, Bernheimer Collection

On an unusual soft blue ground, this carpet has a pattern
which is obviously related to the small Holbein pattern,
but the details of the octagons and crosses are quite
different; the octagons resemble some of those found in
large-pattern Holbein rugs. This pattern could have been
an antecedent of the small Holbein pattern or, more
probably, a less successful competitor. A rug with a rather
similar field pattern, likewise on a soft blue ground,
appears in a picture painted by Antonello da Messina in
Venice about 1476; another closely related pattern is seen
in a rug painted by Memling in Bruges in 1479. The floral
border of the present carpet appears in a regular small-
pattern Holbein carpet painted by Piero della Francesca in
1451 and in large-pattern Holbein rugs, both extant and in
paintings; versions of it persist in later rugs attributed to
Bergama. The interlace border is similar to those of small-
pattern Holbein rugs painted by the Lombard artists
Bergognone, Bernardino de' Conti and Gaudenzio Ferrari
between about 1490 and 1516. Other fragments of the
same or a similar carpet are in the Keir Collection and
the Victoria and Albert Museum, London (acquired in
Italy). A related variant small Holbein pattern appears,
with a similar interlace border, in a rug formerly in the
Dirksen Collection.

Literature
Bernheimer, 1959, no. 143; Erdmann, 1970, pp. 54–5.

Large-pattern Holbein, Memling, Crivelli and Bellini carpets

Large-pattern Holbein carpets (sometimes called Holbein
type III carpets) are so named because they are seen in some
well-known pictures by Hans Holbein the Younger and
because their patterns differ from, and are generally on a
rather larger scale than, that of the small-pattern Holbein
carpet which also appears in one of his paintings. The large
Holbein pattern consists of a grid of rectangular compartments each containing a large octagon or star. This is a very
ancient system of ornament which appears, for example, in
Roman floor-mosaics. It is in fact the same arrangement as
is seen in the animal carpets (nos. 1, 2); the large-pattern
Holbein carpets can be regarded in some respects as successors of these, with the animal groups replaced by abstract
ornament, in line with the general abandonment of animal
motifs in 15th century textile design.

Large-pattern Holbein carpets were exported from Anatolia
to western Europe long before Holbein's time. They are
seen on floors, tables, cupboards, window-sills and boats, in
paintings from Italy, Spain, France, Flanders and England
from about 1460 to 1550 (front endpaper; figs. 7, 19). There
is considerable variety in the details of the designs, much
more so than in the rather standardized small-pattern Holbein
carpets. Most of the rugs depicted are quite small, with only
two rectangles, though larger specimens may have up to four;
examples with more than one rectangle in the width are rare.
These are also the format of the few surviving Turkish
examples (fig. 28 and in museums in Berlin, Istanbul and
Washington, D.C.). Features of these designs persist in later
rugs attributed to Bergama, which can be considered a
possible origin for some of the early pieces also. Turkish
rugs of the large-pattern Holbein type were known in Spain
(e.g. a painting by a Catalan master in the Art Institute of
Chicago) and extensively imitated there during the second
half of the 15th century, probably at Alcaraz and possibly
elsewhere (figs. 29, 30; no. 13). Extant Spanish pieces are
apt to be fairly large, with from three up to thirty rectangles.
The octagons of the large Holbein pattern were also imitated
in needlework made in northern Europe, e.g. an example
of 1539 from Alsace in the Leipzig Museum and another
16th century piece, possibly English, in the Victoria and
Albert Museum (fig. 31).

Besides the major groups of small-pattern and large-
pattern Holbein carpets which were evidently exported from
Anatolia to Europe in large numbers from the middle of the
15th century onwards, a few other types which appear in
paintings of the period are sometimes known by the names of
the artists who painted them. Memling, for example, painted
several different rugs whose patterns include a characteristic
hooked motif, often known by his name (fig. 18; no. 14).
Crivelli is associated with rugs whose principal motif is a
large and complex star (no. 15). A certain type of prayer rug
is associated with Giovanni Bellini (no. 16). These rugs were
evidently made and exported in far smaller quantities than
the Holbein carpets and it is doubtful whether any very
early examples of the Memling and Crivelli patterns are
extant, though they can be recognized in later rugs. A few
early rugs of the Bellini type have survived.

Literature
Ferrandis Torres, 1933; Bode & Kühnel, 1955, pp. 29–32; Ellis, 1963;
Dimand, 1973, pp. 177–9, 254–7; Yetkin, 1974, pp. 64–70; Mackie, 1979,
pp. 91–3.

13

14 Rug with Memling motif

fragments

Anatolia, second half 15th century or later
In two pieces: L. 62 cm. W. 93 cm. and L. 107.5 cm. W. 93 cm.
Budapest, Museum of Applied Arts (Iparmüvészeti
Muzeum), no. 14427
REPRODUCED IN COLOUR PAGE 35

Rugs with patterns of octagons containing stepped lozenges
with hooked outlines appear in a miniature painted for
King René of Anjou about 1460 and in several paintings
by Memling, active in Bruges 1465–94 (fig. 18). The rugs
in the paintings, however, have the motifs arranged in
straight ranks and files, not in offset rows as in this
example. These fragments and another fragment in the
Konya Museum have been assigned to the 15th century,
but they could well be of somewhat later date. The motif
recurs in later Turkish rugs attributed to Bergama and in
Caucasian rugs. The border pattern in the Budapest
fragments is also found in later rugs attributed to Bergama.

Literature
Batári, 1982, no. 1.

14

13 Large-pattern Holbein rug

Southern Spain, second half 15th century
L. 203 cm. W. 123 cm.
London, Victoria and Albert Museum,
no. 784–1905

In this Spanish version of the large Holbein design,
rectangles with plaitwork backgrounds enclose octagonal
frames containing stars with various diaper patterns on
their rays. Other Spanish carpets with this type of design,
generally attributed to Alcaraz, are in museums in New
York, Philadelphia and Washington, D.C; one formerly in
Berlin was destroyed in 1945. Turkish rugs with octagons
enclosing stars of various kinds appear in European
paintings, e.g. in a miniature of about 1460 by the Maître
du Coeur d'Amour Epris, but no exact Turkish prototype
of this Spanish design is known. There is perhaps some
relationship between the stars of twenty-four points in the
Spanish carpets and the sixteen-pointed star of the
Turkish Crivelli pattern, depicted by that artist in 1486
(see no. 15). But the diaper patterns on the stars, and the
border pattern, which recurs in several of these carpets,
seem characteristically Spanish.

Literature
Kendrick, 1915, pl. XXXVII.

15 Crivelli rug

fragment

Anatolia, second half 15th century or later
L. 164 cm. W. 60 cm.
Budapest, Museum of Applied Arts (Iparmüvészeti
Muzeum), no. 14940
REPRODUCED IN COLOUR PAGE 35

Like the dragon-and-phoenix rug and the Marby rug (nos. 1, 2) this unique fragment shows two repetitions of a roughly octagonal motif on a yellow ground. In this case the motif is a complex sixteen-pointed star formed of angular compartments, some of which contain birds and stylized quadrupeds, reminiscent of the earlier animal rugs. A small rug of very similar type, likewise with a yellow ground, appears in paintings of 1482 and 1486 by Crivelli, in Frankfurt and the National Gallery, London. In these paintings, however, the stylization of the birds and other details is different from that of the Budapest fragment and it is possible that the latter, though it has been assigned to the 15th century, is a somewhat later version of the pattern. Another version appears in a still later rug in the same museum (inv. no. 50.127.1). The border design of the present fragment, a lattice of serrated leaves, recurs in a large-pattern Holbein rug in Istanbul and in later rugs attributed to Bergama.

Literature
Batári, 1982, no. 2.

15

16 Prayer rug of Bellini type

Anatolia, late 15th or early 16th century
L. 170 cm. W. 124 cm.
Berlin, Staatliche Museen Preussischer Kulturbesitz,
Museum für Islamische Kunst, no. 87,1368
REPRODUCED IN COLOUR PAGE 38

The rug on which the Muslim kneels to pray inherits traditions which go back to the early days of the faith. Its design is based on that of the mihrab, the niche in the wall of the mosque which indicates the direction of Mecca, towards which the faithful pray. The lamp (restored and barely recognizable in this example) which hangs by a chain from the apex of the arch, recalls a passage in the

16

Quran: 'God is the light of the heavens and the earth. The symbol of his light is a niche wherein is a lamp . . .' Thus the design symbolizes the Divine Presence in the universe or in the heart of man. Even the decorative medallion in the middle of the rug has a long history; the mihrab in the cave beneath the Dome of the Rock, which may go back to the late 7th century, has an eight-petalled rosette in the centre. The octagonal outline at the foot of this and other rugs has been variously interpreted: it may be a niche within a niche, as in some mihrab designs (Zick), or a basin for ablution before prayer, with a water-channel to feed it (Enderlein), or a stylized mountain, as in Chinese dragon robes, so that the worshipper stands symbolically upon elevated ground (Ellis). Though the religious symbolism can have had no appeal for Christian buyers, rugs of this and related types were evidently exported to western Europe in some numbers; they appear in Venetian and other north Italian paintings fairly frequently from the 1490s to the 1520s, then rarely down to the middle of the century (figs. 9, 10). One of the earliest examples is a painting by Gentile Bellini in the National Gallery, London; a rug with a field design very like that of the present example appears in a painting by Giovanni Bellini, dated 1507. The pseudo-Kufic border in the Berlin rug belongs to a type current in the late 15th and early 16th century; it is seen in almost identical form in early Lotto rugs (no. 31). The little flowers set obliquely in the field are reminiscent of motifs from Mamluk and para-Mamluk carpets.

For other prayer rugs see nos. 19, 46–8, 54, 55, 85.

Literature
Zick, 1961; Spuhler, forthcoming catalogue of the Berlin Carpet Collection.

Cairene carpets in the Mamluk style

A large and impressive group of carpets, most of which have been found in Italy, and a few in Austria, Germany and Spain, is readily distinguishable from the Anatolian and Spanish groups. Firstly, their designs, though based on the ubiquitous octagon, are not endless repeating patterns, but are centralized on a large and dominant octagonal medallion, with a great variety of smaller motifs arranged around it. In large carpets there may be three or even five octagonal medallions in the length, but they are of different designs and disposed symmetrically about the single central medallion. Although the motifs are of Near Eastern character, and in some cases specifically Egyptian, these compositions about a central medallion reflect an influence from Persian carpets. Secondly, this group of carpets differ from Anatolian and Spanish carpets in technique; their wool is S-spun instead of Z, they are knotted with the asymmetrical Persian knot instead of the symmetrical Turkish or the Spanish single-warp knot, and their red dye is lac instead of madder. When in good condition, the sheen of their wool, their kaleidoscopic designs, and their colours, often limited to red and light tones of blue and green, give them a special magic, unlike that of any other carpets. One sumptuous example, from the Imperial Collection in Vienna, is knotted in silk.

Examples with heraldic blazons (no. 18) link the group with the Mamluk Empire of Egypt and Syria, which fell before the Ottoman onslaught in 1516–17, but the generally accepted designation of the whole group as Mamluk carpets is apt to be misleading, since many, perhaps most, were probably produced under the Ottomans. It has long been thought that the carpets were made in Cairo, which is known to have been active as a carpet weaving centre by the second half of the 15th century; the Venetian diplomat Barbaro, visiting Tabriz in 1474, remarked that the carpets he saw there were superior to those of Bursa and Cairo. A sound documentary basis for the Cairo attribution is provided for the first time by the newly discovered Mamluk carpet from the Pitti Palace, which is unequivocally identified as a Cairene carpet in a 16th century Medici inventory (no. 21). The Mamluk carpets clearly reflect the environment of a flourishing and luxurious city with international links. Many were of large size, and some very large (no. 21); some of square or circular shape (nos. 22–4) seem to have been specially made for export to Europe, for use on tables. The work of the designer was clearly considered to be important and the designs of the carpets were very varied, even though the repertory of motifs was fairly small. This, again, accords with practice in Persia, rather than Turkey, where commercial workshops reproduced identical repeating patterns over long periods.

The large scale and complexity of the Mamluk designs unfortunately made them rather unsuitable subjects for painters. There are interesting examples in a painting of 1507 by Giovanni Bellini and in wall-paintings in Brescia, ascribed to Moretto or his school and datable before 1543 (back endpaper); otherwise there are only a few unsatisfactory renderings during the second half of the 16th century, down to about 1601. With so little help from the paintings, the chronology of Mamluk carpets remains extremely uncertain. One may postulate a line of development from more abstract to more naturalistic designs, but there are no fixed

points. The development presumably began some time in the second half of the 15th century and ran on until the Mamluk designs were finally replaced by Ottoman designs some time during the second half of the 16th century.

Mamluk carpets do not seem to have been extensively copied elsewhere, though one or two foreign versions are known. C. G. Ellis has suggested (orally) that the carpets in the Brescia wall-paintings might be Italian imitations.

Literature
Recent contributions, with references to the copious earlier literature, are Atil, 1981, pp. 225–7, 242–8; King, Pinner & Franses, 1981; Mills, 1981; Whiting, 1981; Unger, 1982.

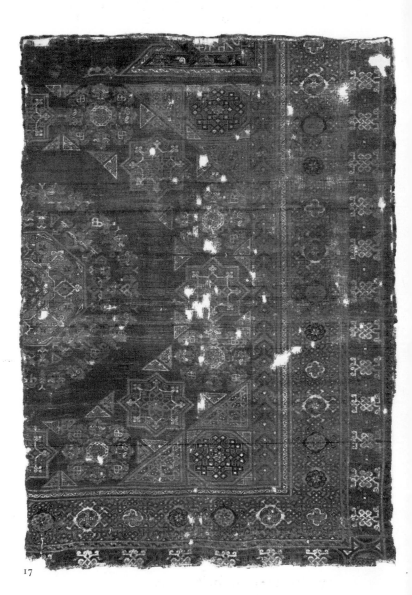

17

17 Mamluk carpet

fragment

Egypt, Cairo, second half 15th century
L. 218 cm. W. 153 cm.
London, Victoria and Albert Museum, no. 150–1908

Formerly with Giuseppe Salvadori of Florence, who acquired it in Italy, this is a battered corner fragment from a large carpet, probably about six metres by three originally, assuming three compartments in the length. It has the usual technique and many of the usual design features of Mamluk carpets, but is unusual in several respects. There is a rather large amount of plain ground in an unusual muted red, which is, however, dyed with the usual lac dye. Some of the commonest Mamluk carpet motifs, such as the umbrella-leaves, are notably absent. Other motifs seen here, e.g. interlace octagons reminiscent of the small Holbein pattern, are rare or unparalleled in Mamluk carpets, but resemble characteristic motifs of Anatolian rugs. Among these is the pseudo-Kufic outer border, which is closely related to 15th century Anatolian models (e.g. fig. 28; no. 8 and a carpet in Istanbul). An Anatolian pseudo-Kufic border of rather different type is seen on a Mamluk carpet painted by Giovanni Bellini in 1507. Charles Grant Ellis has grouped the London fragment with other unusual pieces in the Mamluk manner which he suggests may have been woven elsewhere in North Africa. But technically it is much closer to normal Mamluk carpets than it is to some other members of the Ellis grouping and it seems more probable that it belongs to an early stage of Mamluk carpet weaving in Cairo, before the workshops there had fully developed their characteristic style. Its nearest relation is the Washington fragment (no. 18) which is datable between 1468 and 1516. Is this perhaps the type of Cairo carpet that Barbaro compared unfavourably with those of Tabriz in 1474?

Literature
Ellis, 1967; King, Pinner & Franses, 1981, pp. 36, 38, 42.

18 Mamluk carpet

fragment

Egypt, Cairo, late 15th or early 16th century
L. 220 cm. W. 210 cm.
Washington, D.C., The Textile Museum, no. 1965.49.1

Acquired from a dealer who obtained it in Italy, this fragment of what must have been a very large carpet, nearly four and a half metres wide, is particularly important for the heraldic blazon which appears on it.

18

This composite blazon, which also appears on another carpet, and in embroidery and metalwork, is known to have been used by the Mamluk Sultans Qaitbay (1468–96), Janbalat (1500–01) and Qansuh al-Ghuri (1501–16) and by members of their court. The fragment has many affinities with the London piece (no. 17), for example the design of the principal medallion, the large area of plain red ground, the border of interlace and the presence of elements derived from Anatolian rug-designs. But in the Washington piece the Anatolian influence is far less apparent and the all-over patterning with rows of many small motifs comes closer to the more usual types of Mamluk carpets. If our assumptions are correct, this represents a slightly later stage in the evolution of Mamluk carpet-design than the London piece.

Literature
Ellis, 1967.

19 (detail)

19 Mamluk prayer rug

Egypt, Cairo, early 16th century
L. 162 cm. W. 120 cm.
Staatliche Museen zu Berlin, Islamisches Museum, no. 88,30
(Not in exhibition)

The only surviving prayer rug in the Mamluk style, this is a refined and stately design, which seems to reflect an artistically more cultivated milieu than the strikingly handsome, vigorous style of the nearly contemporary Anatolian prayer rug (no. 16). The present piece shows affinities with the earliest Mamluk carpets (nos. 17 and 18) in the large area of plain red pile and in the design of the outer border and guard stripes; a similar border is seen in a Mamluk carpet painted by Giovanni Bellini in 1507. The little ewer suspended in a bush in the centre of the field lends support to Volkmar Enderlein's suggestion that the octagonal outline at the foot represents a water-basin for ablution before prayer. The umbrella-leaves of the bush and the cypresses and palm-trees in the panel above the arch, stylized though they are, reflect a tendency in Mamluk carpet-design to move away from rectilinear abstract motifs towards more curvilinear and naturalistic effects. The border of cloud-bands, a Chinese motif transmitted to the Islamic world by the Mongols, foreshadows those of many 16th century Anatolian rugs (e.g. nos. 43, 46).

Literature
Ellis, 1969, pp. 5, 20 note 6; Enderlein, 1971.

20 Mamluk carpet

incomplete

Egypt, Cairo, first half 16th century
L. 196 cm. W. 130 cm.
Staatliche Museen zu Berlin, Islamisches Museum, no. 91, 26
(Not in exhibition)

Acquired in 1891 in Munich, this is a fine specimen of the small Mamluk carpets which, to judge from those still extant, must have been exported to western Europe in very considerable numbers, although surprisingly little evidence of this has so far been found in documents or paintings. This piece repeats some of the small motifs seen in the Washington fragment with a Mamluk blazon (no. 18) but the tendrils with umbrella-leaves, which made an appearance in the prayer rug (no. 19) have now entirely overrun the medallion border and the main border. The carpet is particularly notable for its rich and beautiful colour.

Literature
Erdmann, 1970, fig. 188.

20

21 The Medici Mamluk carpet

Egypt, Cairo, first half or middle 16th century
L. 1088 cm. W. 409 cm.
Florence, Palazzo Pitti, no. 5279
REPRODUCED IN COLOUR PAGE 41

This extraordinary carpet, found only a few months ago in the store-rooms of the Pitti Palace, constitutes, together with the Ottoman carpet from the same source (no. 56), the most remarkable discovery of recent times in the field of Oriental carpets. We are deeply indebted to the Italian authorities for permitting these two carpets to be displayed to the public for the first time in this exhibition.

The first salient fact about this carpet is its gigantic size. It is one of the largest of all Oriental carpets, even longer than the Ardabil carpet in the Victoria and Albert Museum, London (fig. 32), though not so wide. A second salient fact is its almost perfect condition. It allows us to see the repertory of Mamluk ornament deployed on a scale unequalled elsewhere, in a carpet intended for a palace, and in virtually the same condition as when it was first delivered to the Grand Duke Cosimo I de' Medici. A third and very important fact about the carpet is that it can be traced back in the Medici archives to its arrival, some time between 1557 and 1571, in the *Guardaroba Granducale di Palazzo Vecchio*, where it was described as a Cairene carpet, '*Tappeto Cairino lungo b. 19 e largo b. 7*'; the abbreviation *b.* denotes the Florentine *braccio* of about 58 cm. The nearly perfect condition both of this carpet and of the Ottoman carpet from the same collection is no doubt due to the fact that they were always classified as 'reserve carpets', signifying no doubt that they were never to be exposed to ordinary use, but were to be brought out only to adorn the very grandest of state occasions. The custodians of the Medici collections from the 16th century to the present day are to be congratulated on their success in preserving these enormous carpets in almost pristine condition.

As in many Mamluk carpets the colours of the woollen pile are limited to three, with the pattern in blue and green on a red ground. In the centre is a huge octagonal medallion with eight rays or spokes projecting from its rim. At each end is a very large eight-sided medallion of another type; by some miscalculation in the weaving, one of these medallions is a little misshapen. Each medallion occupies an approximately square section of the field and is surrounded by its own satellite system of octagons, octofoils, stars, triangles, parallelograms and other geometrical figures, in a kaleidoscopic multiplicity which defies description. These vast octagons and complex geometric patterns suggest notions of infinity and the cosmic diagrams of Buddhist thought. It is hardly likely that carpets were meant to be read as philosophical or religious maps, but it is possible that such ideas lay somewhere in the background of Mamluk carpet design, if only in the form of remote design-influences from Central Asia or the Far East.

The main border with a pattern of cartouches is of a type common in Mamluk carpets; similar borders are seen in wall-paintings attributed to Moretto or his school, datable before 1543 (back endpaper). The guard stripes with foliage patterns are also common. The inner border of interlace recalls early Mamluk carpets (nos. 18, 19).

The arrival of this carpet in the Medici collection

between 1557 and 1571 is a new fact which may well be significant for the chronology of Mamluk carpets. Of course it may not have been absolutely new at that time, but these dates lend support to the idea that carpets in the pure Mamluk style were still being woven until the middle and perhaps even the third quarter of the 16th century.

The compiler of this note wishes to thank Signora Lucia Ragusi, who discovered the relevant documents, and Signor Alberto Boralevi, who allowed access to his article on the carpet prior to publication.

Literature
Boralevi, 1983.

22 Mamluk carpet

Egypt, Cairo, first half or middle 16th century
L. 265 cm. W. 240 cm.
Vienna, Österreichisches Museum für angewandte Kunst, no. T 8346

Formerly in the Imperial Collection in Vienna, this is an excellent example of the approximately square carpets which were exported to Europe, perhaps mainly for use on tables. In the fully developed Mamluk style, it has many points of resemblance with the similarly shaped Boston carpet (no. 23); among many other similarities, note that the pattern of the guard stripes is the same (the outer guard is missing from the present piece). But notwithstanding their similarities, the composition of the designs differs in many respects, and this is characteristic of Mamluk carpets. The Egyptian workshops constantly reshuffle their relatively limited repertoire of motifs to produce an endless variety of designs, unlike many of the Anatolian workshops which reproduce the same repeating patterns for generations. A border pattern similar to that of the present example, with a cross-motif in the middle of the cartouche, appears in Mamluk carpets in wall-paintings at Brescia, attributed to Moretto or his school, datable before 1543 (back endpaper).

Literature
Sarre & Trenkwald, 1926, pl. 47.

21

22

23 Mamluk carpet

23

Egypt, Cairo, first half or middle 16th century
L. 269 cm. W. 279 cm.
Boston, Museum of Fine Arts, no. 61.939;
Harriet Otis Cruft Fund
REPRODUCED IN COLOUR PAGE 40

This carpet first appeared in the V. and L. Benguiat sale
at the American Art Association in 1932; its earlier history
is unknown. Apart from some reknotting, mainly in the red
areas, it is in splendid condition, with a full and luxurious
pile, and with the web ends and warp fringes still present.
As in many Mamluk carpets, the square shape of the
main field composition has been extended to an oblong
rectangle by the addition of extra bands of ornament.
These additions are usually made at the ends of the field,
but in this and a few other examples they are made at the
sides, so that the carpets are wider than they are long – a
rare format for carpets. The design is in the developed
Mamluk style with a full complement of umbrella-leaves
and lancet-leaves and with cartouche borders. Adolph
Cavallo has pointed out that it is especially closely related
to carpets in museums in New York and Vienna,
suggesting that they must have been woven at about the
same time, or perhaps even in the same workshop. Among
other similarities, he stresses the pseudo-Kufic ornaments
in the central medallion, which are suggestive, like many
pseudo-Kufic inscriptions in carpets, of the name of Allah.

Literature
Cavallo, 1962; Denny, 1978, p. 158.

24 Circular Mamluk carpet

Egypt, Cairo, first half or middle 16th century
Diameter 287 cm.
Private Collection

Formerly in the collection of Piero Barbieri, Genoa, this
carefully restored piece is unique among Mamluk carpets
for its circular shape. But evidently there was a continuing
demand for circular carpets from Cairo, for there is one in
the later, Ottoman style in the Corcoran Gallery of Art,

Washington, D.C., and another is said to be in the
Archbishop's Palace at Kremsier. No doubt these carpets
were special export orders, intended for use on the circular
tables which were popular in western Europe. There is a
relevant entry in the 1596 inventory of Archbishop
Ferdinand of Austria, referring to 'two handsome Cairene
carpets, the gift of the Doge (?) of Genoa, with many
colours and . . . yellow fringes, for use on round tables'.
The present carpet is in the fully developed Mamluk style,
with its panoplies of umbrella-leaves and lancet-leaves. It
is interesting to see how the designer has tackled the
problem of fitting a pattern devised for rectangular carpets
into a circle. The field design works reasonably well apart
from slight awkwardness at the edge, but the cartouche
border looks decidedly uncomfortable.

Literature
Erdmann, 1970, p. 198; Sotheby's, London, 12th October 1982, lot 38.

24

25

Other Holbein, Para-Mamluk and Compartment carpets

Besides the Mamluk carpets, a number of others have related designs of large octagonal medallions or stars, with smaller octagons and other motifs grouped about them. Some of these carpets are entirely Anatolian in their technique and their design-motifs and are closely related to the large-pattern Holbein carpets. There are several examples in Istanbul and one in Munich (no. 26); a comparable piece is the unique Soumak carpet in Washington, D.C. (no. 27). The standard form of the design, with a large medallion in the middle and two smaller medallions at each end, appears in a painting of 1494 by Mansueti (page 105) and in works by other Italian painters down to the middle of the 16th century. Designs of this kind, sometimes referred to as Holbein type IV, persisted in later rugs attributed to Bergama.

Exactly the same type of design is found in another group of carpets, which are technically unlike normal Anatolian rugs (nos. 28, 29). They are made, not with the Turkish symmetrical knot, but with the same asymmetrical knot as the Mamluk carpets, and they also include some Mamluk details – notably rows of small trees and plants – in the design; they have been called para-Mamluk carpets. On the other hand, the materials (madder dye, not lac, and Z-spun wool, not S-spun as in Mamluk carpets) and the major part of the designs seem to be Turkish, so that it is generally supposed that the carpets must have been made in Anatolia, in workshops founded by craftsmen trained in the Mamluk tradition. Rugs thought to belong to the para-Mamluk group have been noted in Italian paintings from 1501 to 1555 (fig. 11). Similar technical features and a simplified version of the para-Mamluk octagon design appears in the so-called compartment or chequerboard carpets (no. 30), which are seen in Italian and northern European paintings of the late 16th and early 17th centuries and have survived in considerable numbers.

Literature
Kühnel & Bellinger, 1957; Erdmann, 1961, pp. 102–5; Ellis, 1963; King, Pinner & Franses, 1981; Mills, 1981; Whiting, 1981.

25 Mamluk carpet
incomplete

Egypt, Cairo, first half or middle 16th century
L. 387 cm. W. 277 cm.
Washington, D.C., The Textile Museum, no. R16.3.1

Acquired in 1925 from A. Loewi, Venice, this is the battered remains of an imposing carpet which, assuming three compartments in the length, must have been over six metres long. It has a number of unusual features, notably the awkward rectangle of the end compartment. The designer seems to have assembled rather heterogeneous motifs, which he has not succeeded in combining into an integrated composition. The delicate curvilinear leafy lattice of the inner border and the little palmettes in the frame of the rectangle, suggestive of a fairly advanced date in the 16th century, sit oddly alongside the abstract motifs of an older generation. Yet this carpet has many features in common with the great silk Mamluk carpet in Vienna. Kühnel ventures to suggest that these two, together with the Simonetti, Bardini and Bernheimer Mamluk carpets, may have been produced in the same manufactory.

Literature
Kühnel & Bellinger, 1957, pp. 35–6, pls.XIX, XX; Ellis, 1962, pp. 40–1.

26 Carpet with large and small medallions
incomplete

Anatolia, late 15th or early 16th century
L. 350 cm. W. 217 cm.
Munich, Bayerisches Nationalmuseum, no. 10/294

This much damaged carpet with two large star-medallions belongs, together with other examples in Istanbul, to a group which is related on the one hand to Anatolian large-pattern Holbein carpets and on the other to para-Mamluk rugs such as no. 28. The centre of the carpet is missing and it is possible, though not certain, that it included two more small octagons like those which appear at each end. One of the end borders has a pseudo-Kufic pattern similar to that found in small-pattern Holbein carpets of the second half of the 15th century (nos. 6, 7) and in various rugs in Italian paintings from 1459 to 1507. The borders on the other three sides recur in a 16th century needlework carpet in the Victoria and Albert Museum, London (fig. 31) and, in simplified versions, in carpets in Istanbul. A carpet with two closely comparable star-medallions and a field pattern very like this appeared in Holbein's 1537 portrait of Henry VIII and his family at Whitehall Palace; the border in that case was the type of interlace border commonly found in small-pattern Holbein carpets from the 1520s onwards. A Spanish carpet with a design related to that of the present piece was in the collection of Count Wilczeck.

Literature
Erdmann, 1955, fig. 45; Ellis, 1963, pp. 7–8.

26

27

27 Soumak carpet with large and small octagons

Anatolia or the Caucasus, late 15th or early 16th century
L. 300 cm. W. 176 cm.
Washington, D.C., The Textile Museum, no. 1961.2.1

This extensively damaged and repaired carpet is unique. It is not a knotted-pile carpet, but is executed in the so-called Soumak technique of weft-wrapping, which is a very ancient tradition in the Near East and elsewhere, but which is primarily associated with 19th century carpets from the Caucasus area. No other Soumak carpet of this type and period is known. The details of the field design are quite closely related to those of the large-pattern Holbein carpets and to carpets such as no. 26; the stars-and-bars pattern of the octagons and the foliate pattern of the border of the large octagon are almost identical with those of the star-medallions in the latter. The cross-motifs in the field are very like those in a painting of 1479 by Memling. The border pattern of interlace appears on a rug painted by Francesco Morone in 1503, in Venetian paintings of small-pattern Holbein carpets down to the 1540s and in an English carpet of 1603 (figs. 8, 27).

Literature
Ellis, 1963.

28

Anatolian borders generally have plain butt-joints. Rugs very similar to this one are seen in paintings by Sophonisba Anguissola dated 1555, etc. A related but perhaps somewhat later rug, with a similar border, is in the collection of C. G. Ellis. (Mackie, 1973, no. 24; *Hali*, II, no. 1, 1979, colour plate V opposite p. 56).

Literature
Erdmann, 1961, p. 104, note 256; Ellis, 1963, pp. 5–6; Dimand, 1973, pp. 180–2.

29 Para-Mamluk rug with large and small octagons

fragment

Anatolia, second or third quarter 16th century
L. 45 cm. W. 98 cm.
Washington, D.C., The Textile Museum, no. R34.32.1

This is a small fragment of a rug which, like the larger pieces in the C. G. Ellis and former Campana collections, seems to represent an intermediate stage between no. 28 and compartment rugs such as no. 30. The fragment is part of one end of the rug, with two small octagons, and the edge of the central compartment which would have contained a larger octagon. In these rugs the octagons consist of several rows of small trees and plants arranged radially around a star of interlace. Such octagon designs have antecedents among early Mamluk carpets, e.g. the large fragmentary carpet from the Imperial Collection in Vienna, and cf. nos. 17, 18. Related but not identical rugs are seen in Italian paintings and in a Flemish tapestry from the second quarter of the 16th century.

Literature
Kühnel & Bellinger, 1957, pls. XLV, XLVI.

28 Para-Mamluk rug with large and small octagons

Anatolia, first half 16th century
L. 178 cm. W. 125 cm.
Philadelphia Museum of Art, no. '55–65–2;
The Joseph Lees Williams Memorial Collection

The layout of this rug, with a large octagon in the centre and a pair of smaller octagons at each end, is found in a number of typically Anatolian pieces, such as no. 26. This example, however, belongs to a different group, which is knotted with the asymmetric knot, like the Mamluk carpets, and borrows some small motifs – rows of cypress trees and stiff flowers – from the Mamluk repertory (cf. nos. 17, 18). Charles Grant Ellis has called them para-Mamluk carpets. But the materials used are apparently Turkish, not Egyptian (Z-spun wool, not S-spun; madder dye, not lac), and most of the design is in a pure Turkish style. The carpets were presumably woven in Anatolia by workshops manned initially by craftsmen trained in the Mamluk tradition, but using local materials and designs. The design of the octagons and other details of the present rug resembles those of nos. 26 and 27. The pseudo-Kufic border is related to various types found in small-pattern Holbein rugs of the second half of the 15th century and in Lotto rugs of the first half of the 16th century. But notice that the border pattern here is turned neatly round the corners of the rug, as in Mamluk carpets, whereas

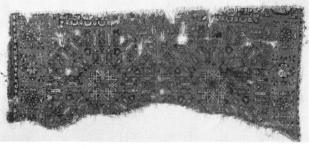

29

30 Compartment rug

Anatolia, late 16th or early 17th century
L. 192 cm. W. 140 cm.
Vienna, Österreichisches Museum für angewandte Kunst, no. T 10512

The so-called compartment or chequerboard rugs are technically very similar to the para-Mamluk rugs and may be considered as part of the same group. The octagons of small radiating motifs which the para-Mamluk rugs had inherited from earlier Mamluk carpets are here reduced to a simple repeating pattern suitable, like the Holbein and Lotto patterns, for mass-production of carpets in all sizes; to judge from the number surviving, compartment rugs were indeed produced in considerable quantities. The octagons are placed in a continuous grid of rectangular

30

compartments, reminiscent of the old large-pattern Holbein designs and, like them, infinitely extensible; an example in the Bardini Museum, Florence, has as many as thirty-two rectangles, but small pieces like the present one are more usual. In this example, as in many others, the triangular panels of ornament in the top corners of the rectangles touch those in the bottom corners, producing an effect of hexagons rather than octagons.

The design of the compartment rugs was the last of the many rug-patterns based on octagons which were devised during the 15th and 16th centuries. These rugs are seen in Italian, English and Dutch paintings chiefly in the last quarter of the 16th and the first quarter of the 17th century, always with the same cartouche border as in the present example; note that the border pattern turns neatly round the corners as in the para-Mamluk rugs. According to family tradition, this piece, which formerly belonged to the Counts Kufstein, was bought in Constantinople in the early 17th century.

Literature
Völker, 1979, p. 14.

Lotto carpets

Lotto carpets are named after the Venetian painter Lorenzo Lotto, who depicted them on more than one occasion, but was by no means the first to do so. In fact they are seen in many Italian paintings from 1516 onwards, in Portuguese paintings from about the 1520s onwards and in northern European, including English, paintings from the 1560s onwards. They continue to appear frequently in paintings, particularly in Holland where they were much used as table-carpets, down to the 1660s and occasionally thereafter.

The design of the Lotto carpets is simple, ingenious and obviously very successful. Executed almost invariably in yellow on red, with blue details, it can be seen as an updated version of the octagons and crosses of the small Holbein pattern, or of the rectangles containing octagons of the large Holbein pattern. But the clear geometric forms of the earlier patterns are here dissolved into meandering tendril-like lines which break out now and then into vaguely leaf-like projections – a kind of half-way house between a geometric and a foliate pattern – with all its elements linked together so that they coalesce in a mazy network. Because of the relationship between their patterns and those of the Holbein carpets, Lotto carpets are sometimes called Holbein type II, though Holbein never depicted them.

In a thought-provoking article, Charles Grant Ellis has distinguished three principal varieties of the Lotto pattern. The most usual version, seen in many paintings from 1516 to the 1660s and in many surviving examples (figs. 11, 21; nos. 31, 32), he calls the Anatolian style, supposing rugs of this kind to have been made in the Konya area, the Ushak area and other places in Anatolia. Another version, more angular than the first, with jagged saw-tooth outlines, is called the kilim style; this, too, appears in many paintings from 1538 to the 1660s, and in extant examples (fig. 23; no. 34). A third variety, the ornamented style, differs from the Anatolian mainly by the addition of extra curlicues (no. 35). It is found in a number of extant rugs, but is difficult to distinguish in paintings; the most likely representations so far noted are in Dutch paintings of the 1640s. Many of the surviving rugs in the kilim style have been found in south-eastern Europe and Ellis suggests that rugs in both kilim and ornamented styles were produced by a cottage industry in that area, not in Anatolia. He further suggests that certain rugs in the Anatolian and kilim styles which appear in Italian paintings from the 1520s onwards may be Italian copies of Lotto rugs; this could also be true of extant fragments with the arms of the Genoese families Centurione and Doria. A number of extant carpets are clearly late 16th or 17th century Spanish copies of the Anatolian and kilim styles. The Anatolian style was also imitated in England in the late 16th century (no. 33). To add to the complexity of the situation, fake Lotto rugs in all three styles have been produced in the 20th century.

Literature
Erdmann, 1970, pp. 57–60; Ellis, 1975; Mills, 1981.

This carpet belongs to a group of large Lotto carpets, of which other examples are in museums in Washington, D.C., and Chicago. It has been shortened and was probably much longer originally; the example in Washington, which is of about the same width, is nearly twice as long. The field pattern of these carpets is of the Anatolian type. Their characteristic border pattern of floral cartouches has not been identified in any 16th century painting, though a greatly simplified version of it is seen in many Lotto rugs depicted in paintings between about 1600 and 1670. This form of border is, however, firmly anchored in the second half of the 16th century by the fact that it is imitated in English Star Ushak carpets dated 1584 and 1585, also at Boughton (no. 37). The large size of the present carpet and others of the same group, together with the elaborate border pattern, which is turned quite neatly round the corners (an unusual feature in Turkish carpets), suggests production in urban workshops with a well-trained workforce, like those which produced the large Ushak carpets. Charles Grant Ellis, however, considers that they have too little in common with the Ushak carpets to permit attribution to the same centre.

Literature
Beattie, 1964, no. 4; Ellis, 1975, pp. 19, 24, 30 note 3.

31

31 Lotto rug

Anatolia, first half 16th century
L. 170 cm. w. 109 cm.
The Saint Louis Art Museum, no. 104:1929; gift of James F. Ballard

Formerly in the James F. Ballard Collection, this rug is said to have come from a Spanish convent. It shows the Lotto pattern in its most usual, so-called Anatolian form, which is seen in many European paintings from 1516 to the 1660s. The pseudo-Kufic border of the present example appears in some of the earliest representations of Lotto rugs, in paintings by Sebastiano del Piombo in 1516, by a Portuguese master in the 1520s and by Lotto in 1542 (fig. 11). Other small Lotto rugs with this border are preserved in museums in London, Paris, New York, Philadelphia and elsewhere; a larger example in Berlin, destroyed in 1945, had a variant of this border pattern which is recorded in a painting of 1561 by Frans Floris. Charles Grant Ellis proposes an attribution to the Konya area for this group of Lotto rugs.

Literature
Dimand, 1935, pl. XXI; Erdmann, 1970, fig. 52; Ellis, 1975, pp. 19, 24, 30 note 1.

32 Lotto carpet

incomplete

Anatolia, second half 16th century
L. 359 cm. w. 245 cm.
His Grace The Duke of Buccleuch and Queensberry, K.T., Boughton no. 4

32

33

33 Lotto rug

England, late 16th century
L. 178 cm. W. 134 cm.
His Grace The Duke of Buccleuch and Queensberry, K.T.,
Boughton no. 5.

Lotto rugs were occasionally woven with a blue ground
instead of the usual red, e.g. rugs depicted in Flemish
paintings of the 1620s and an extant example in Istanbul
(Yetkin, 1974, colour plate 35). The present example
shows the Anatolian version of the pattern in tan on blue.
The tonality of the dyed wools, however, is different from
that of Turkish rugs, and the warp and weft are of flax,
not wool as in Turkey. The colours and materials are very
like those of the Star Ushak carpets dated 1584 and 1585,
also at Boughton (no. 37), and it seems probable that this
rug was produced by the same weavers and at about the
same time as those. The Star Ushak carpets are woven
with the arms of Montagu and various initials, presumably
of the weavers, and the whole group is generally believed
to have been made in England, like several other carpets of
the late 16th and early 17th centuries with English arms.
There is documentary evidence for the production of
Turkey carpets in England at that time and an inventory of
1588 attributes one, of about the same size as the present
piece, to Norwich. A Netherlandish origin has sometimes
been suggested for these carpets (Beattie, 1964), but there
seems to be no real basis for this. The border pattern of
the present piece is one which is generally associated with
Ushak rugs (fig. 16; no. 47); it is seen on a Lotto rug,
however, in a portrait painted in Italy in 1598.

Literature
Tattersall, 1934, p. 36, pl. IV A; Beattie, 1964, no. 3; Ellis, 1975, pp. 28–9.

34 Lotto rug

Anatolia or south-eastern Europe, late 16th or first half
17th century
L. 165 cm. W. 114 cm.
Budapest, Museum of Applied Arts
(Iparmüvészeti Muzeum), no. 14433
REPRODUCED IN COLOUR PAGE 37

Lotto rugs in the kilim style, the more angular version of
the pattern, with characteristic saw-tooth outlines, are
seen in Italian paintings from 1538 onwards, but much
less frequently than those in the Anatolian style. Between
1611 and 1667, however, they appear in English paintings
as floor-carpets and in Dutch paintings as table-carpets,
and were evidently as common as the Anatolian variety
(fig. 23). Many extant rugs in the kilim style have been
found in south-eastern Europe. Charles Grant Ellis has
suggested that they were produced by a cottage industry
in that area and may have been traded up the Danube and
down the Rhine to supply the northern European markets;
this interesting theory has not yet been supported by
documentary evidence. Kilim-style rugs in English and
Dutch paintings have cartouche or cloud-band borders;
the ragged palmette border of the present piece does not
seem to be represented, though it occurs on other extant
kilim-style rugs. A similar border pattern appears on
various rugs in Italian and English paintings from the
1520s onwards, including an Anatolian-style Lotto rug
painted by Girolamo dai Libri in 1530; the very stiff
version of the pattern seen in the present piece is probably
of considerably later date.

Literature
Batári, 1974, no. 3.

34

35

35 Lotto rug

Anatolia or south-eastern Europe, first half 17th century
L. 155 cm. W. 114 cm.
Wher Collection, Switzerland

This rug shows the rarest version of the Lotto pattern, the ornamented style, which resembles the Anatolian style, but with variations and additions, chiefly extra curlicues. It is not easily recognized in paintings; the most likely examples so far noted are in paintings of the 1640s by J. G. van Bronckhorst, which have cartouche borders similar to those of the present rug. Other extant rugs with ornamented fields and cartouche borders are in museums in Paris, New York and elsewhere. This type of cartouche border, which may be regarded as a simplified version of the 16th century type seen in no. 32, appears on many Lotto rugs, in both Anatolian and kilim styles, in English and Dutch paintings from about 1605 to 1665. Lotto rugs in the ornamented style have been found in south-eastern Europe and Charles Grant Ellis has suggested that they, like the kilim-style rugs, were produced by a cottage industry in that area.

Star Ushak carpets

Ushak, a small town in the interior of western Anatolia (the modern spelling is Uşak, but carpet literature still retains the old phonetic spelling) is recorded as an important centre of carpet production from the 17th century onwards. It is customary to attach its name to a very large proportion of Anatolian carpets produced from the 16th century onwards, but it is probably wiser to regard this, not as an attribution, but simply as a useful label adopted for classification purposes, just as the names of Holbein and Lotto have been annexed to other types. The common denominators of the so-called Ushak carpets are a palette based on a strong red and a deep blue, and designs combining arabesque and plant ornament in compositions, inspired in part by Persian models, which are far more free and flowing than the earlier geometric patterns. In addition to large carpets with various designs, generally classified as Star Ushak and Medallion Ushak carpets, there are also Ushak prayer rugs.

The introduction in the early 16th century of the Lotto pattern, in which geometrical figures are outlined by meandering tendrils and leaf-like forms, was symptomatic of a relaxation of the former geometrical discipline of Anatolian rug design. The Star Ushak pattern, which first appears in a painting of 1534 by Paris Bordone, completes the stylistic revolution (nos. 36, 37). It is based, like many of the older patterns, on an alternation of two motifs, in this case a large star-like motif of eight points and a smaller lozenge; these motifs, in deep blue, are filled with arabesques. The alternating motifs are not packed close, as in earlier patterns, though a certain reluctance to let them float free is manifested by the linkages between all motifs in the same horizontal row. Instead, extensive areas of red ground are opened up between the motifs and lightly overlaid with arrangements of stems and flowers, contrasting with the formality of the arabesques. There is a clear relationship between this pattern and Persian designs such as that of the Ardabil carpet, with its floral ground, and its arabesque-filled medallions and ovals (figs. 32, 33). Even though the Ardabil carpet, dated 1539, is slightly later than the first Star Ushak carpets, there can be no doubt that the latter were devised under Persian influence. This influence could well have arrived through peaceful channels, but it was quite probably reinforced by Ottoman occupation of parts of Persia, including the important carpet weaving centre of Tabriz in 1514 and from 1533 onwards. Unlike the Persian medallion designs, however, the Star Ushak design is conceived as a repeating pattern, usable for carpets of any size, from quite small to very large.

Star Ushak carpets appear in European paintings from 1534 until the second quarter of the 17th century and were evidently exported to Europe in considerable numbers; they were also copied in Europe (no. 37). In addition to the usual Star Ushak design, a number of other attractive designs in similar style and colouring were current at the same period (nos. 38–40).

Literature
Bode & Kühnel, 1955, pp. 38–40; Erdmann, 1963; Yetkin, 1974, p. 81 ff.

36

36 Star Ushak carpet

Anatolia, late 16th or early 17th century
L. 322 cm. W. 193 cm.
The National Trust, Hardwick Hall

The earliest recorded appearance of the Star Ushak pattern
is in a carpet which lies before the Doge's throne in Paris
Bordone's painting of 1534 in the Accademia, Venice. The
present piece, a characteristic example of the type, forms
part of the furnishings of Hardwick Hall in Derbyshire,
which was built between 1591 and 1597. It is not certain
that it belonged to the original furnishings of the house,
but it is by no means impossible. Floral borders very
similar to the one seen here appear on a variant Star Ushak
carpet in a posthumous portrait of Henry VIII (fig. 14) and
on a Medallion Ushak carpet in a painting of the English
royal family, about 1570. Star Ushak carpets were evidently
popular in England, witness the English copies of 1584–5
at Boughton (no. 37) and carpets seen in English portraits
of 1611–18 attributed to William Larkin and Marcus
Gheeraerts. Other examples appear in paintings by
Zurbarán, dating from the second quarter of the 17th
century. A carpet resembling the present one, with a
similar border pattern, is in the Kunstgewerbemuseum,
Cologne; other Star Ushak carpets can be found in most
major carpet collections.

Literature
Beattie, 1959, pp. 8–10; Beattie, 1964, no. 2.

37 Star Ushak carpet

England, 1585
L. 274 cm. W. 183 cm.
His Grace The Duke of Buccleuch and Queensberry, K.T.,
Boughton no. 2

This carpet, dated 1585 on the web end, is one of three
matching Star Ushak carpets at Boughton House,
Northamptonshire, one of which, dated 1584, is much
larger, 561 × 244 cm., while the third, undated, is rather
smaller, 254 × 131 cm. In the centre of the border on each
side of the three carpets is a shield with the arms of

Montagu impaling Harington, referring to the marriage
of Sir Edward Montagu of Boughton (1532–1602) and
Elizabeth Harington, ancestors of the present owner.
Except for a slight elongation of the motifs, the carpets
reproduce the Star Ushak pattern quite accurately. The
colours, however, differ from those of Turkish Star Ushak
carpets and the use of flax for the warp and weft – not
wool, as in Anatolia – point to a European origin. It has
been suggested that these carpets might have been
produced in the Netherlands (Beattie, 1964), but there
seems no good reason to seek an origin outside England.
There are several other carpets of the late 16th and early
17th centuries with English heraldry and with technical
characteristics similar to these. There is also ample
documentary evidence for the production of Turkey
carpets in England at that time; the Earl of Leicester's
inventory of 1588 attributes one specifically to Norwich.
Letters woven into the Boughton carpets, mainly in the
borders, are thought to be the initials of the weavers; the
present rug has the letters A N in the border and E B in
the field. The small Lotto rug at Boughton (no. 33)
resembles these Star Ushak pieces in many respects and
was presumably made in the same workshop.

The border design of the Star Ushak pieces is similar to
that of the large Anatolian Lotto carpet at Boughton
(no. 32). The guard stripes resemble those of the Ushak
prayer rug (no. 47).

Literature
Tattersall, 1934, p. 36, pl. II B.

37

38

38 Variant Star Ushak carpet

fragments

Anatolia, 16th or early 17th century
L. 290 cm. W. 168 cm.
London, Victoria and Albert Museum, no. 278–1906

These fragments illustrate a comparatively rare variant of the Star Ushak type in which the four points of large cross-shaped motifs are linked diagonally to the corners of indented rectangular motifs, so as to form horizontal and vertical compartments containing a lozenge motif disposed horizontally or vertically. The various motifs, which contain arabesques, form a rather dense network, leaving only a limited area of ground free for floral ornament. The complex and ingenious layout appears a little confused in the present patchwork assemblage; the effect might be improved if a section at one end, made up of several fragments patched together, could be removed to the opposite end. Carpets of this design are generally fragmentary or in poor condition: other examples are in museums in Berlin, New York, Philadelphia, Saint Louis and elsewhere.

Literature
Erdmann, 1963, pp. 89–94.

39 Variant Star Ushak carpet

Anatolia, 16th or early 17th century
L. 506 cm. W. 156 cm.
Harold Mark Keshishian Collection

A rare variant of the Star Ushak design is based on the

alternation of two main motifs, a foliated eight-pointed star and a straight-edged eight-pointed star, both dark blue and containing arabesque and plant ornament, on the usual red ground with a floral pattern. The present piece, in an unusual long and narrow format, is the principal example known; apart from this and a small carpet in the Philadelphia Museum of Art there are only one or two others. A few other surviving carpets renounce the alternation of motifs and repeat only one of the two star forms, generally the foliated star. Carpets of this class appear in two well-known posthumous portraits of Henry VIII, from the middle or second half of the 16th century; the one in the Walker Art Gallery, Liverpool (fig. 14), shows only the foliated star, while that at Belvoir Castle shows both stars, but less accurately. The main border of the present carpet is lost, except for a small section at one end; it appears to be a version of the arabesque and floral border seen in nos. 33 and 47.

Literature
Pope, 1926, no. 38; Erdmann, 1963, pp. 83–8; Mackie, 1973, no. 39.

39

40

40 Variant Star Ushak carpet

incomplete

Anatolia, 16th or early 17th century
L. 315 cm. W. 229 cm.
The Saint Louis Art Museum, no. 98:1929; gift of James
F. Ballard

This piece was in the 1925 V. and L. Benguiat auction and
subsequently in the collection of James F. Ballard.
Though cut at both ends and repaired, it remains one of
the most beautiful of Ushak carpets, with particularly
rich and deep colouring. Its design, which appears to be
unique, is based on a single repeated motif, a very large
dark blue quatrefoil, containing an unusually elaborate and
stately composition of arabesques and plant ornament, and
with six small arabesque finials radiating from it. The red
ground is sprinkled with flowers of the usual Ushak type.
The large scale and freshness of this carpet allows us to
appreciate the designer's work more directly than in some
other Ushak carpets where the vivacity of the original
conception has been a little dulled by frequent repetition.
The border, a variant of the arabesque and floral border
seen on nos. 33 and 47, is also found in other Ushak
carpets.

Literature
Dimand, 1935, pl. XVI.

Medallion Ushak carpets

The largest and grandest of the Ushak designs is that of the
Medallion Ushak carpets, which makes its earliest appearance in a painting of the English royal family, at Sudeley
Castle, about 1570. Obviously inspired by Persian medallion
carpets, it is none the less in most respects thoroughly
Turkish in feeling. Comparison with Turkish tile-work
suggests that the original design was made about the second
quarter or middle of the 16th century. Though on a very
large scale, the design is treated as a repeating pattern based
on the alternation of two main motifs. One is a large pointed
oval medallion which invariably appears in the centre of the
carpet, sometimes with part of another similar medallion
appearing at each end. The other is a composite star-like
medallion of sixteen points (as seen in earlier Persian medallion carpets such as no. 59), which invariably appears at
the sides of the carpet, so that only about half of any example
is visible. Both types of medallion are filled with compositions
of arabesques and plant ornament. Both have large finials
projecting from the ends and the star-like medallion also has
smaller finials projecting at the sides. The ground, which is
quite restricted in relation to the large size of the medallions,
is covered with a restless pattern of stems, leaves and lotus-
flowers, apparently inspired by Chinese textile patterns.
There is hardly a straight line anywhere in the design – a
remarkable and revolutionary change from the rigid geometry
of older Anatolian rugs! The design is eclectic, masterly,
majestic, indeed a stupendous performance. In the last
analysis it might be said to lack contrast, balance and repose,
but these were not, perhaps, the qualities which were most
highly prized in Oriental carpet design.

At all events, the design was immensely successful. Medallion Ushak carpets were evidently exported in great
numbers and they are to be seen in paintings from most
western European countries – in works, for example, by
Zurbarán, Velasquez, Vermeer and Terborch – down to the
second half of the 17th century, and even occasionally in the
18th. They came in many varieties. Some of the earliest and
best of the extant examples have a dark blue ground with
ivory flowers, the oval medallion in red and the star-like
medallion in blue (no. 41). Others have a red ground (as in
the painting of 1570) with blue flowers and dark blue
medallions. Ivory medallions are also found (Berlin and the
Keir Collection). The design was modified and simplified in
various ways. Copies were produced in Europe – in Spain
and in Poland (no. 42). Versions of the pattern continued to
be made in Anatolia down to the 19th century, some of them
perhaps in the Ushak area, which might provide some
justification for the attribution of the earlier carpets to that
area also. But on the whole it seems wiser to regard the
Ushak designation simply as a convenient group-name, not
as an attribution, for which the evidence is negligible. Wher-
ever they were made, the weaving of the large Medallion
Ushak carpets, with their immensely complex and continuously curvilinear designs, must have required large and
well-organized workshops, presumably in a flourishing urban
environment.

Literature
Bode & Kühnel, 1955, pp. 34–42; Yetkin, 1974, pp. 75–81.

73

medallions at the sides, and a deep blue field overrun with lotus trails in ivory. It shows well the two long interlacing serpentine lines which underlie the composition and bind it together, each line following the contour of one side of the red medallion, then swinging across to touch the facets of the blue medallion on the opposite side of the field before swinging back again to follow the outline of the next red medallion. The carpet is closely related to two others, in the Hamburg Kunst und Gewerbe Museum and in the former Stroganoff Collection, both of which have the pseudo-Kufic border which appears, partly restored, at one end of this piece. This is probably the earliest of the border patterns found in Medallion Ushak carpets. Pseudo-Kufic borders, common in earlier Anatolian carpets, seem to have gone out of use during the second half of the 16th century. The floral border on the other three sides of this piece, and the inner guard stripe, resemble those of no. 40.

Literature
Beattie, 1972, no. 14.

41 Medallion Ushak carpet

Anatolia, 16th or early 17th century
L. 544 cm. W. 261 cm.
Lugano, Switzerland, Thyssen-Bornemisza Collection, no. 656a
REPRODUCED IN COLOUR PAGE 39

Though rather extensively restored and reknotted with puffy new wool, particularly in the bright blue, this is none the less a fine early example of the Medallion Ushak type. The design is accurately drawn and is given ample room to develop the full effect of its rich complexity, with the great red medallion at the centre and parts of two more at the ends, with the halves of four light blue star-

41

42

42 Medallion Ushak carpet

Poland, Bialystok, first half 17th century
L. 345 cm. W. 188 cm.
Berlin, Staatliche Museen Preussischer Kulturbesitz,
Museum für Islamische Kunst, no. I.4928

This carpet is an example of the abridged versions of the
Medallion Ushak design which were current in the 17th
century, generally with dark blue medallions and blue
floral trails on a red ground; the original sixteen-pointed
star-medallions are commonly reduced to segments of
twelve-pointed stars. Carpets of this type are seen in Dutch
and other paintings, for example one by Vermeer in the
Royal Collection. Besides those made in Anatolia, copies
were produced in Spain and Poland. This example and its
twin in Wawel Castle, Cracow, bear the arms and initials
of Krzysztof Wiesiolowski, who became Grand Marshal of
Lithuania in 1635 and died in 1637. They differ from
Anatolian examples in various details, such as the coarse
plied wool used for both warp and weft, and are believed
to have been made in a workshop which he set up on his
estates at Bialystok in north-eastern Poland. The will of
his widow in 1649 mentions twenty-four locally made
carpets of Turkish type. The border pattern, like the field,
is copied from an Anatolian original.

Literature
Mańkowski, 1954, pp. 70–3 (on the Cracow piece); Spuhler, forthcoming
catalogue of the Berlin Carpet Collection.

43

White ground carpets

Two groups of Anatolian carpets were habitually produced
with white (or ivory) grounds for both the field and the
border. Both types have remarkably simple and indeed
rather primitive patterns. One is composed of a cluster of
three discs and a pair of parallel wavy stripes (no. 43); these
have been variously interpreted, but are generally thought
to be symbolic representations of the markings on leopard
and tiger skins. The other design consists of some rather
awkwardly drawn plant motifs, including a bird-shaped
arabesque motif which has earned these carpets the name of
bird rugs (no. 44); the motif is based on one which was
extensively used in Istanbul tile-work from the 1560s (Öz,
pls. XLI, XLVI, XLVII). Both designs were employed for
quite large carpets as well as for small rugs. Their border
patterns and other features are similar to those of the Ushak
carpets and they are often attributed to the same centre,
though their elementary field patterns are very different
from the elaborate Ushak designs. A few variant designs and
prayer rugs are also found with white grounds.

Bird carpets are seen in a few European paintings from
the second half of the 16th and the early 17th century. They
were also copied in Europe (no. 45). Indeed, the simple
designs of the white ground rugs are easy to copy and many
fakes have been produced in the 20th century.

Literature
Bode & Kühnel, 1955, pp. 46–8; Yetkin, 1974, pp. 93–100; Mackie, 1976.

43 White ground carpet with spots and stripes

Anatolia, late 16th or early 17th century
L. 315 cm. W. 202 cm.
Washington, D.C., The Textile Museum, no. 1976.10.1;
Purchase, Arthur D. Jenkins Gift Fund and Proceeds from
the Sale of Art

This carpet, which belonged to Wilhelm von Bode from
1901 until his death in 1929, was subsequently acquired
by Robert Woods Bliss and was in the Dumbarton Oaks
Collection. The border at one end is missing, as are parts
of the outer guard stripe on the other three sides; there are
small areas of reknotting. The cluster of three spots was a
well-known textile pattern since the early Middle Ages; it
has been associated with the Buddhist *chintamani* emblem
and with the badge of the Mongol conqueror Timur. The
three spots in association with a pair of wavy lines were a
favourite pattern of Ottoman textiles, embroideries, ceramics
and other arts from the 15th century onwards; it has been
suggested that they refer to the markings of leopard and
tiger skins and were symbols of power. Related motifs also
appear in Cairene carpets (no. 51). In the present example
the pattern is enlivened by random colour variations in the
motifs. Similar carpets are in the Bardini Museum,
Florence, and in the Schwarzenberg Collection (said to be
recorded in an inventory of 1724); others in museums in
London and Berlin have proved to be 20th-century fakes.
Carpets of this type do not appear in western European
paintings. But the cloud-band border seen here appears in
many paintings from 1519 onwards and in many extant
carpets of the Lotto and Ushak types (e.g. no. 46). The
rosette pattern of the inner guard stripe recurs in Cairene
carpets (e.g. no. 49); the vine pattern of the outer guard is
seen in a bird rug depicted by Hans Mielich about 1557.

Literature
Erdmann, 1970, p. 81 ff.; Mackie, 1976.

44

44 White ground bird carpet

Anatolia, late 16th or early 17th century
L. 289 cm. W. 156 cm.
Wher Collection, Switzerland
REPRODUCED IN COLOUR PAGE 37

Formerly in the Mounsey Collection, this piece is an
excellent example of its type, in very fair condition except
for losses at the ends and small repairs elsewhere. The so-
called bird rugs take their name from the bird-like
arabesque or leaf motifs which, attached to round blossoms,
form compartments enclosing a rather clumsy floral spray.
The layout is basically that of the old large-pattern Holbein
carpets or the contemporary compartment carpets, but is
enlivened by the irregular and oblique outlines of the
motifs. Curiously, in the present carpet the whole field
pattern is slightly askew in relation to the side borders.
The shapes of the bird-leaves, the markings on them, and
many other small details vary from one repetition to the
next; at one end of the field the bird-leaves are reversed.
White ground bird rugs are seen in a few western European
paintings from 1557 to about 1625. The present example
has a cartouche border, of which other versions are seen in
Lotto carpets (nos. 32, 35).

45 Green ground bird carpet

fragment

Western Europe, late 16th or early 17th century
L. 86 cm. W. 180 cm.
Wher Collection, Switzerland

A white ground bird rug in a private collection in Stockholm
is woven with the name and ecclesiastical arms of Andreas
Prochnicki, who was Latin Archbishop of Lvov from 1614
to 1633. His predecessor Jan Zamojski is reported to have
ordered twenty carpets with his arms from Istanbul in
1603, but Prochnicki's carpet is suspected of being a copy
woven somewhere in eastern Europe. That bird rugs were
copied in Europe, and not always with white grounds, is
shown by the present fragment. Its colours, its flax warp
and weft, and the patterns of its border and guard stripes
all point to a European origin; England and Spain have
been suggested as possibilities.

Literature
Colour plate of another fragment of the same carpet, *Hali*, IV, no. 3,
1982, p. 78.

45

Ushak, Transylvanian and other prayer rugs

Ushak prayer rugs resemble the larger Ushak carpets in colouring and ornament. A few retain the traditional design of the mihrab arch (no. 46), but far more adopt a symmetrical design based on Persian prototypes (no. 47). Prayer rugs of this kind appear in European paintings from 1519 to 1625 (figs. 12, 16).

Two new types of prayer rug appear in paintings from the 1620s onwards. The type which is more frequently seen is called Transylvanian, since many of the extant examples have been found in that area and adjacent regions (no. 48). These are in some respects the successors of the Ushak prayer rugs and, like them, generally have a symmetrical design with an arch at both ends. Their repertory of ornament, however, is mostly new, probably inspired by Persian models. The second type, of which, once again, many of the extant examples have been found in south-eastern Europe, is quite different (fig. 34). The striking design of three stilted arches carried on six slender columns is derived from another source – a class of prayer rugs produced in Cairo and in the so-called Ottoman Court workshops. Because the columns are arranged in two pairs, as well as two single columns, rugs of this type have been called coupled-column prayer rugs. Both the Transylvanian and the coupled-column type are generally thought to have been woven in Anatolia. Charles Grant Ellis, however, has suggested that they may have been produced in south-eastern Europe.

Literature
Bode & Kühnel, 1955, pp. 43–4, 48–53; Beattie, 1968; Vegh, Layer and Dall'Oglio, 1977, pls. 9–16, 23–8.

46 Ushak prayer rug

Anatolia, 16th century
L. 156 cm. W. 100 cm.
Paris, Musée des Arts Décoratifs, no. 10423

This rug was given to the museum by Jules Maciet in 1902. The angular arch and plain spandrels have an archaic air, suggestive of an old and austere tradition. The central medallion is very similar to that of the early Anatolian prayer rug in Berlin (no. 16), while the angular outline below is an attenuated version of those which appear both in that rug and in the Mamluk prayer rug (no. 19) and are sometimes interpreted as representations of a water-basin and a canal supplying it. The cloud-band border also recalls the Mamluk rug. Cloud-band borders and outer guard stripes very similar to those seen in the present rug appear in a painting of 1519 by Girolamo da Santacroce and in a portrait of Queen Mary I (1553–8) with her father, at Althorp (and cf. figs. 12, 20). Similar cloud-band borders recur in rugs of various types down to the 17th century (e.g. no. 43).

Literature
Bode & Kühnel, 1955, p. 44.

47 Ushak prayer rug

Anatolia, late 16th or early 17th century
L. 155 cm. W. 113 cm.
Budapest, Museum of Applied Arts
(Iparmüvészeti Muzeum), no. 24459

46

47

This rather battered and repaired rug retains the central medallion and stylized lamp of the early Anatolian prayer rug (no. 16), but the lamp is now the only directional feature which remains in a design which is otherwise completely symmetrical, in the manner of Persian medallion-and-corner designs. The corners are filled with quarter-sections of large quatrefoils, forming a semblance of an arch at both ends of the field. Within the quarter-quatrefoils are arabesque compositions similar to those which are a feature of the large Ushak carpets; some other rugs of this class have cloud-bands in place of the arabesques (cf. fig. 16). The rich border pattern of arabesques and stylized plants was current in the late 16th century (cf. no. 33). Another rug with almost identical field, border and guard stripes is in the Protestant church at Braşov, Romania. Besides pieces such as these, in south-eastern Europe, other examples of the class have been found in Italy; all together, a rather large number seem to have survived, but it may well be that some of these are 20th century reproductions. Double-ended prayer rugs of this and related types are seen in European, chiefly Italian, paintings from 1519 to 1625; they are sometimes called Tintoretto rugs since they appear in the work of that master.

Literature
Batári, 1974, no. 2; Vegh, Layer & Dall'Oglio, 1977, no. 9; Batári, 1982, no. 14.

48 Transylvanian prayer rug

Anatolia, early 17th century
L. 172 cm. W. 132 cm.
Budapest, Museum of Applied Arts
(Iparmüvészeti Muzeum), no. 7967

A few Transylvanian prayer rugs have an arch at one end only, but most, like this one, which is an outstanding example of its class, have a symmetrical design with an arch at both ends, as did the Ushak prayer rugs. The arabesque corner pattern seen here is also found in some of the Ushak rugs (no. 47). In other respects this design represents a new departure for Anatolian prayer rugs. There is a lamp at both ends which, however, is treated as a flower vase, from which spring floral stems, overrunning the whole of the unusual blue field; this floral composition is not fully symmetrical, suggesting that it was adapted from one originally devised for a prayer rug with a single arch. It does not appear to be related to the floral designs of prayer rugs produced in Cairo (no. 54); the character of the flowers rather suggests a Persian prototype, but this has not yet been identified. The characteristic border pattern of angular cartouches and the guard stripes with their reciprocating trefoil certainly reflect the influence of Persian models (cf. fig. 13). Rugs of this type appear as table-carpets in western European paintings from 1620 onwards (fig. 22); a good example, very similar to this one, is seen in Thomas de Keyser's portrait of Constantijn Huygens, dated 1627, in the National Gallery, London. Examples at Skokloster, Sweden, are said to have been brought back from the East by Count Wrangel in 1653. Variants of the type were produced over a long period; some from Transylvanian churches bear 18th-century dedication dates and examples appear in 18th-century paintings, both in Europe and in the American colonies. Transylvanian rugs are generally attributed to Anatolia, often to Bergama, but Charles Grant Ellis suggests that they may have been made in south-eastern Europe. Imitations have been produced in Romania in the 20th century.

Literature
Vegh, Layer and Dall'Oglio, 1977, no. 12.

48

Cairene carpets in the Ottoman style

The large group of extant carpets in the rectilinear Mamluk style, which are attributed to Cairene workshops of the late 15th and the first half of the 16th century, were succeeded by another large group, identical in technique, but in the very different curvilinear Ottoman style, with flowers and curling feathery leaves. Some of the changes, for example the introduction of medallion-and-corner designs (nos. 51, 53), were no doubt stimulated by the example of Persian carpets, but the details of the new designs are characteristically Ottoman, in a style which is closely paralleled in the tile ornaments of the buildings of Istanbul from the middle of the 16th century onwards. This style is so utterly different from the Mamluk style that there can be no question of a gradual transition from one to the other, but some early Ottoman carpets have the same restrained colour scheme as many Mamluk carpets (no. 49) and occasionally motifs from the two styles are uneasily juxtaposed, as for example in a carpet with an entirely Mamluk field and a fully developed Ottoman border (Erdmann, 1961, fig. 9).

Carpets in the Ottoman style are technically identical to the Mamluk carpets and are made with the asymmetrical Persian knot, not the symmetrical Turkish type. It is reasonable to suppose that, like the Mamluk carpets, they were made in Cairo. The designs, however, are so like those of the tile-work in Istanbul that it is natural to enquire whether some designs may have been supplied from this city, and indeed whether some of the carpets may have been woven there. An interesting Turkish document indicates that in 1585 Sultan Murad III requested the Governor of Cairo to send eleven master carpet weavers and a quantity of wool to the court at Istanbul. A finely woven prayer rug of the early 17th century, formerly in the Sultan Ahmet Mosque at Istanbul, has long been labelled there as Istanbul work; unlike most carpets in the Ottoman style, which are entirely in wool, it has a silk warp and weft and its woollen pile is supplemented with cotton. It has been suggested that this and a number of other pieces made with the same materials (nos. 54, 55) form a separate group which may be attributed to court workshops in Istanbul or, alternatively, in the silk-weaving centre of Bursa. But this hypothesis rests on a very insecure basis. Cairo was not averse to using silk for finer pieces, witness the silk Mamluk carpet in Vienna, and other Cairene silk carpets are mentioned in 17th century inventories in Europe and Istanbul. The silk fringes of Cairene carpets described in the 1596 inventory of the Archduke Ferdinand of Austria suggest the presence of silk warps, and the newly available evidence of the great carpet from the Pitti Palace (no. 56), which was described in 1623 as a Cairene carpet, yet has cotton in the pile, deals a fatal blow to the theory that carpets with this material were a prerogative of Istanbul or Bursa. This does not necessarily mean that no carpets in the Ottoman style were woven in Istanbul, Bursa, or elsewhere, but simply that they cannot be distinguished from Cairene carpets by the criteria hitherto proposed.

An alternative theory, propounded by M. S. Dimand, that all carpets in the Ottoman style were probably made in Istanbul or Bursa, and not in Cairo, is likewise controverted by the evidence of the Pitti Palace carpet. There is ample documentary evidence that considerable numbers of Cairene carpets were exported to western Europe and to Istanbul during the late 16th and 17th centuries, but there is virtually no comparable evidence of carpets exported from Istanbul or Bursa.

Many carpets in the Ottoman style have been found in Italy and elsewhere, but unfortunately the complex patterns of these carpets were not often recorded in paintings. Without assistance from this source, their chronology remains somewhat uncertain. It is sometimes alleged that two silk caftans in Istanbul, said to have belonged to Sultan Beyazid II (1481–1512), prove that the Ottoman style seen in the carpets was already fully developed at the beginning of the 16th century, but these caftans are obviously mislabelled and can hardly be earlier than the second half of the century. Comparisons with dated tile-work in Istanbul suggest that the earliest carpets in the Ottoman style are of about the middle or third quarter of the 16th century (no. 49). Most of the pieces exhibited probably date from the late 16th or early 17th centuries (nos. 50–5). The newly discovered carpet from the Pitti Palace, which was presented to Grand Duke Ferdinando II in 1623, adds a valuable new piece of chronological evidence (no. 56). With its immense size and immaculate condition it also allows us to see for the first time the original effect of a great palace carpet of this type.

Carpets in the Ottoman style were copied in Spain and in Poland.

Literature
Kühnel & Bellinger, 1953; Erdmann, 1961; Dimand, 1973, pp. 196–205; Denny, 1979; King, Pinner & Franses, 1981.

49

49 Ottoman rug

Egypt, Cairo, third quarter 16th century
L. 193 cm. W. 137 cm.
London, Victoria and Albert Museum, no. 458–1884

Acquired from a collection in Italy in 1884, this rug has exactly the same restrained colouring – limited to red, blue and green – as many pieces in the Mamluk style which are assigned to the first half of the 16th century. The design retains no Mamluk elements, but is probably one of the earliest examples of the pure Ottoman style. The field design, a favourite in Ottoman carpets, is based on repetition of a single motif, a quatrefoil of arabesques, flowers and feathery leaves; there is a rosette between the quatrefoils, and each quatrefoil is linked to its neighbours by a slender floral stem. The beautifully drawn border shows palmette-shaped cartouches, carnations and leaning tulips. The rosette pattern of the guard stripes is seen in other Ottoman and Anatolian carpets.

Literature
King, Pinner & Franses, 1981, pp. 36, 43.

50 Ottoman carpet

fragments

Egypt, Cairo, late 16th or early 17th century
L. 227 cm. W. 232 cm.
Paris, Musée des Arts Décoratifs, no. 5127

Bought from Stora in 1889, this is an assemblage of fragments from a larger carpet, of which other fragments are in museums in Cairo, London, Stockholm and Washington D.C. The design is based on the repetition of a large pointed oval medallion in blue, enclosing a quatrefoil of arabesques and flowers; successive medallions in the length of the carpet are linked by small white lobed medallions. The red field is occupied by a splendidly vigorous repeating pattern of flowers and very long curling feathery leaves. Charles Grant Ellis has compared the layout to those of Persian carpets attributed to Kashan and Kerman. The borders of the present assemblage are less than half the width of the original borders; fortunately, the border fragments on three sides show the lower part of the

border pattern, while that on the fourth side shows the upper part. The complete border pattern was similar to that of no. 49, but considerably more elaborate. Besides this main border, fragments of the same carpet in other collections show minor borders and guard stripes (the latter also present here), making up a total border width of around 90 cm., which suggests a carpet of very large size. Ellis's reconstruction proposes dimensions of about 9 metres long and 5 metres wide, almost comparable with the Ardabil carpet (fig. 32). But the format of the newly discovered carpet from the Pitti Palace (no. 56) suggests the possibility of a rather long and narrow carpet, with the complete field only a few centimetres wider than that of the present piece. A carpet with a related medallion and field pattern, but a different border, appears in a portrait of Charles I as Prince of Wales, at Parham Park, painted by Daniel Mytens in 1623.

Literature
Ellis, 1962.

51 Ottoman rug

Egypt, Cairo, late 16th or early 17th century
L. 197 cm. W. 129 cm.
Paris, Institut de France, Musée Jacquemart-André
(Not in exhibition)

This is one of a set of four matching rugs, of similar size, which are said to come from the Palazzo Corsi in Florence; the other three are in museums in Berlin, Budapest and London. A fifth, apparently identical piece is in the Metropolitan Museum of Art, New York. In the centre of the rug is a blue pointed oval medallion with finials, recalling that of no. 50, and in the corners there are quadrants with arabesques. The pattern of spots and wavy stripes which covers the field is thought to be a symbol of power, inspired by the markings of leopard and tiger skins. Pieces in Berlin, Cairo and London show that this pattern was also used by the Cairene weavers for prayer rugs and for larger carpets; the London fragment has a border pattern related to those of nos. 49 and 50. Another version of the spots-and-stripes pattern was current in

50

52

Anatolian carpets at the same period (no. 45). The border pattern of the present rug and the other matching pieces consists of two interlacing floral stems, with the unusual feature that not only the corner blossoms but also those in the centre of each side are specially oriented. This border recurs in other Ottoman carpets (e.g. Beattie, 1968, fig. 3; Dimand, 1973, no. 106); comparable border patterns are seen in Istanbul tile-work of the 1560s and 1570s (Öz, pls. XXXVIII, XLIV).

Literature
Erdmann, 1961, pp. 96–7; Beattie, 1968, fig. 4.

52 Ottoman table-carpet

Egypt, Cairo, late 16th or early 17th century
L. 241 cm. W. 254 cm.
London, Victoria and Albert Museum, no. 151–1883.

Bought in Paris in 1883, this cruciform table-carpet and another with coats of arms in the San Gimignano Museum,

together with fragments of a third in Berlin, were no doubt specially made for export to Europe, like the earlier circular table-carpets from Cairo (no. 24). While the other two examples retain traces of Mamluk design, this one is purely Ottoman. The red ground has a pattern of quatrefoil motifs in blue and green, like the early example no. 49. In addition, the main and side panels of the carpet have polychrome floral roundels, and cartouches resembling those in the border of the prayer rug, no. 54; the large roundel in the main panel, like other such roundels in Ottoman carpets (e.g. Dimand, 1973, no. 102), shows ragged wavy stripes interlaced with the flowers – evidently larger versions of the wavy stripes in no. 51. The border pattern, a favourite Ottoman type, has long curving leaves, with lotus and other blossoms, on an undulating stem; the use of a similar border in conjunction with a field pattern in pure Mamluk style (Erdmann, 1961, fig. 9) suggests that it was current by the third quarter of the 16th century.

Literature
King, Pinner & Franses, 1981, pp. 36, 46–7.

53

53 Ottoman carpet

Egypt, Cairo, late 16th or early 17th century
L. 251 cm. W. 201 cm.
Wher Collection, Switzerland

This carpet was in the 1925 Benguiat sale in New York
and the 1970 Kevorkian sale in London. It is an excellent
example of the small carpets in rather squarish format
which the Cairene weavers continued to produce in the
Ottoman style as they had done earlier in the Mamluk
style; no doubt they served mainly as table-carpets in
Europe. This one has a green floral medallion in the
centre and dark blue quadrants with cloud-band ornament
in the corners; compartments with cloud-bands of related
type are seen in Istanbul tile-work about 1600 (Öz, pl.
LIV). The red field has a typical repeating pattern of
flowers and twisting leaves. The main border is a more
ample version of that seen in the preceding table-carpet,
no. 52. The minor borders have the same pattern as the
guard stripes of no. 50. The little reciprocating pattern
in the guard stripes here is also found in Persian carpets
(e.g. no. 86).

Literature
Sotheby's sale catalogue, London, 11th December, 1970, lot 5.

54 Ottoman prayer rug

Egypt, Cairo, late 16th or early 17th century
L. 180 cm. W. 125 cm.
Baltimore, The Walters Art Gallery, no. 81.4

This prayer rug is one of a group which, unlike the all-
wool carpets which are generally attributed to Cairo, have
a silk warp and weft, and a pile which includes light blue
and ivory cotton as well as wool. They have sometimes
been attributed to Ottoman court workshops in Istanbul
or Bursa, but their designs are indistinguishable from
those of Cairene carpets. The whole field design of the
present rug, including the arch, recurs in technically
similar prayer rugs in museums in Vienna and New York
(the latter, however, has no cotton in the pile). The opulent
floral design beneath the arch, quite Baroque in its ripeness
and movement, though a little blunted by extensive
reknotting in this example, is also seen in the repeating
patterns of larger Ottoman carpets, including all-wool
Cairene carpets. The quadrants with cloud-bands also
recur in other Ottoman carpets (e.g. no. 53), as does the
border with cloud-bands and floral cartouches (cf. Dimand,
1973, no. 102). The patterns of the minor borders and
guard stripes are frequently seen in Cairene carpets.

Literature
Ellis, 1969, p. 5 ff.; Ettinghausen and others, 1974, no. 11.

54

55

55 Ottoman prayer rug

Egypt, Cairo, early 17th century
L. 172 cm. W. 127 cm.
Staatliche Museen zu Berlin, Islamisches Museum,
no. 89,156
(Not in exhibition)

This battered but still beautiful rug belongs, like no. 54, to the group of finely knotted carpets, with silk warp and weft, and with the woollen pile supplemented with light blue and ivory cotton; these pieces have often been attributed to Ottoman court workshops in Istanbul or Bursa. Other prayer rugs of this group, with similar major and minor borders and similar guard stripes, are in museums in Budapest, Istanbul, New York and Vienna; the Istanbul piece was formerly in the Sultan Ahmet Mosque, built in 1617. A related but anomalous example in Berlin, without cotton, is said to be dated AH 1019 (AD 1610–11) in a chronogram. The border pattern of these rugs is perhaps a relatively late type of Ottoman border; it recurs in the Pitti Palace carpet (no. 56) which may date from about 1620. The present rug, like the Budapest piece, has a plain red field beneath an elegant arch carried on two slender columns; these or similar rugs were the prototypes for a series of Anatolian Ghiordes rugs of the 18th and 19th centuries. The elegant floral pattern of the arch-spandrels here is not known in other examples.

Literature
Ellis, 1969, p. 5 ff.

56 The Medici Ottoman carpet

Egypt, Cairo, early 17th century
L. 995 cm. W. 330 cm.
Florence, Palazzo Pitti, no. 5278
REPRODUCED IN COLOUR PAGE 41

Together with the Mamluk carpet, also from the store-rooms of the Pitti Palace (no. 21), this Ottoman carpet forms part of the most remarkable discovery of recent years in the field of Oriental carpets and we are privileged, through the generous co-operation of the Italian authorities, to present it to the public for the first time in this exhibition. As the largest and best preserved of all Ottoman carpets, it allows us to judge the original effect of this style in a palace carpet of enormous size. Moreover it is precisely documented in the *Guardaroba Granducale di Palazzo Vecchio*, which describes it as a Cairene carpet and indicates that Duke Ferdinando II received it in 1623 from Admiral Verrazzano: '*Tappeto grande Cairino buono lungo b.17 e largo b.5 e 2/3, avuto dal Gen. Cav. Da Verrazzano Commissario delle Galere addi 31 luglio*'; the abbreviation *b.* denotes the Florentine *braccio* of about 58 cm. One wonders whether Admiral Verrazzano obtained it by way of trade or in the course of naval operations.

The pile of the carpet, in addition to wool in five colours, includes large amounts of white and light blue cotton, as in the prayer rugs nos. 54, 55. The prayer rugs have a silk warp and weft, whereas this huge carpet not surprisingly has a wool warp and weft, but the contemporary identification of it as a Cairene carpet effectively undermines the theory, prevalent hitherto, that the carpets with cotton in the pile were made in Ottoman court workshops in Istanbul or Bursa and not in Cairo.

The design of the carpet is simple, based on the repetition of a single large motif, a green quatrefoil with feathery leaves and flowers, extended at each end by repeating one lobe of the quatrefoil; the red ground is covered with more feathery leaves and flowers. This is a stretched version of a favourite Ottoman carpet design, seen already in the earliest examples (no. 49). It is undeniably impressive over the vast length of this carpet, but there is a certain clumsiness at the junctions of adjacent motifs; the Cairene workshops, though extremely efficient carpet producers, were perhaps less effective on the design side at this period. But this design was evidently well-liked, since it was copied in Anatolia (Victoria and Albert Museum, London, no. T136–1909). The main border pattern is found in other 17th century Ottoman carpets (e.g. no. 55) and versions of it persisted in Anatolian Ghiordes carpets until the 19th century. The pattern of the minor borders is seen in Istanbul tile-work from the 1560s (Öz, pl. XXXV) and in other Ottoman carpets (e.g. the carpet of which no. 50 is a fragment). The S-shaped motif of the guard stripes appears not only in Ottoman carpets (e.g. no. 55), but in others from the 15th century onwards (e.g. no. 1). It is remarkable that the present carpet still retains its striped web ends.

The compiler of this note is indebted to Signora Lucia Ragusi, who discovered the relevant entry in the Medici archives, and to Signor Alberto Boralevi, who permitted consultation of his article on the carpet prior to publication.

Literature
Boralevi, 1983.

56

PERSIAN AND INDIAN CARPETS
Medallion and cartouche carpets

The designs of Persian carpets owe much to the miniaturists and other practitioners of the arts of the book, which were highly developed in Persia. Designs having a central medallion with ornaments projecting at each end (nos. 59, 60, 62) and designs with a medallion in the centre and quarter-medallions in the corners (no. 58) were seen, for example, in bookbindings long before they appeared in carpets. Persian miniature paintings, which frequently depict carpets, suggest that until the late 15th century Persian carpets generally had repeating patterns related to those of Anatolian Holbein carpets, but no examples of this type have survived. In miniatures of the 1480s attributed to Bihzad, much larger and freer types of design make their appearance, including medallion carpets (no. 57 ff.) and cartouche carpets (no. 61).

Medallion designs dominated carpet making in Persia in the 16th century and medallion carpets were no doubt made in all the major carpet weaving centres. Many of them have been attributed to north-west Persia and particularly to Tabriz, the capital of the Turkoman rulers of the area in the 15th century and of the Safavid Shahs of Iran from 1502 onwards. During the first half of the 16th century, however, the whole area, including Tabriz, was repeatedly attacked and occupied by the Ottoman Turks. There is general agreement that carpets such as nos. 57 to 59, which include Turkish details and have the medallion simply superimposed on top of a repeating pattern, were made in north-west Persia. They are splendidly impressive and monumental carpets, but they have an air of being rugged, commercial and perhaps rather provincial simplifications of subtler and more refined designs. A carpet such as no. 60 is a possible prototype for the medallion and field pattern of no. 58.

The finest 16th century carpets of Persia were no doubt specially designed by skilled painters and they represent the supreme achievement of the art. As far as we can tell, such carpets were produced in an edition of one, or sometimes in a matched pair, as was the case with the Ardabil carpets of 1539/40 (fig. 32) or the cartouche carpets (no. 61, another design which was subsequently adapted for commercial production in north-west Persia). Nos. 62 to 64 are examples of medallion carpets designed by painters in various Persian centres – possibly Tabriz, Herat and Kerman. In these, as in the Ardabil carpets and other great artist-designed carpets of the period, the field is occupied, not by a repeating pattern, but with compositions of flowers, animals and landscapes, specially designed in relation to the medallions and other ornamental forms. It must not be assumed that the designs of these great carpets are merely ornamental; they also have symbolic meanings and are, in some sense, visions of paradise. This is an aspect which cannot be adequately explored in a few words and interested readers are advised to consult the writings of Professor Cammann.

Inventories and other documents indicate that Persian carpets were arriving in Europe in considerable numbers from the second half of the 16th century and possibly earlier. Not surprisingly they seem to have been valued at much higher rates than the ordinary grades of Turkish carpets. Some of the medallion carpets exhibited here are known to come from old European collections (nos. 58, 62). Persian medallion carpets are also seen in European paintings, for example, in a portrait of the Duke of Buckingham, dated 1626, by Daniel Mytens; further study of such paintings may well provide useful information for the chronology of the carpets.

Literature
Pope, 1939, III, p. 2283 ff.; Bode & Kühnel, 1955, pp. 80–107, 116–23; Erdmann, 1955, pp. 30–3; Dimand, 1973, pp. 38–50; Cammann, 1972 and 1975.

57

57 Medallion carpet

North-west Persia, late 15th or 16th century
L. 516 cm. W. 214 cm.
Boston, Museum of Fine Arts, no. 65.595; William Francis Warden Fund

This large and complete though severely worn carpet, woven entirely in wool, is of particular interest for the early date assigned to it by recent research. The repeating pattern on the red field is based on the alternation of two motifs, one a quatrefoil with leaves and lotus flowers, the other a star of interlace also surrounded by lotus flowers; there are two colour schemes for each motif, used in alternate rows. Despite many differences in detail and in general effect this pattern is clearly related to the small Holbein pattern which was current in Anatolian carpets from 1451 or earlier. Perhaps both were descended from a common ancestor; prototypes of such patterns are seen in Persian miniatures from the late 14th century onward. Professor Denny compares the details of the large blue floral medallion, rimmed by Chinese-inspired clouds, with embroidery designs made for the Turkoman court at Tabriz in the 15th century and, for this and other reasons, suggests that the carpet was woven in the Turkoman principalities of north-west Persia before the end of that century. Could this have been one of types of carpets that Barbaro admired in Tabriz in 1474? The floral patterns of the border and guard stripes are perhaps not entirely incompatible with such a date, though one would have supposed them to be later. The design of the central medallion recurs, with different field patterns, in north-west Persian carpets of later date in museums in Glasgow and Paris. Did this sixteen-lobed medallion influence the eight-lobed medallions of Mamluk carpets?

Literature
Denny, 1978, pp. 156–7; Denny, 1982, p. 332.

58 Medallion carpet

North-west Persia, 16th century
L. 530 cm. W. 222 cm.
Lisbon, Calouste Gulbenkian Museum, no. T.97
REPRODUCED IN COLOUR PAGE 42

Formerly in the Imperial Collection in Vienna, this carpet has sometimes been associated with the Emperor Charles V; the date is about right, but there is no other evidence. It is one of the finest of a group of surviving carpets, woven with a woollen pile and cotton warp and weft, which are generally attributed to north-west Persia and often to Tabriz; other examples are in museums in London, New York, Washington, D.C. and elsewhere. These are large carpets in a long and relatively narrow format (one in the Metropolitan Museum of Art, New York, is more than 12 metres long) with a central star-shaped medallion of sixteen points and sometimes, as here, with smaller quarter-medallions in the corners, all superimposed on a repeating pattern of arabesques and coiling floral stems in groups of four. In the present example the coiling-stem pattern is particularly well drafted, fits the width of the field exactly and stands out very clearly against the green ground – the usual ground colour of these carpets is red. The central star-medallion looks like a squared-up version of a circular sixteen-pointed star such as that of no. 60;

58

59 Medallion carpet

North-west Persia, 16th century
L. 545 cm. W. 184 cm.
Washington, D.C., The Textile Museum, no. R33.1.2

Formerly in the Von Tucher Collection, this is a fine
example of the north-west Persian group of medallion
carpets, closely related to that from the former Imperial
Collection, now belonging to the Gulbenkian Foundation
(cat. no. 58). The repeating pattern on the green ground is
very similar, though somewhat curtailed at the sides in
this narrower carpet. The sixteen-pointed star-medallion
in the centre differs from that of the Gulbenkian carpet,
though the same Anatolian octagon and star appear at
the centre. The medallion here is similar to the star-
medallions of Medallion Ushak carpets; it has a cartouche
and finial above and below, but there are no corner-
medallions. The arabesque border is a very characteristic
north-west Persian type.

Literature
Bode & Kühnel, 1955, pp. 81–2.

edged with cloud-like cresting, it is mainly red, with a
pattern of flowers and eight small birds; at the very centre
is an octagon enclosing a star of a kind often seen in
Anatolian carpets. The corner medallions are of similar
type, but smaller in scale and less assertive in colour. The
bold border pattern of flowers and red strapwork on a
dark blue ground in quite characteristic of these carpets.
Carpets of this class, made in the frontier area of north-
west Persia, must have been, of all Persian carpets, the
most readily accessible for the Ottoman Turks and may
well have influenced Anatolian carpet design; there is a
relationship, for example, between the sixteen-pointed
star-medallions of these carpets and those of the Medallion
Ushak design.

Literature
Pope, 1939, pl. 1122; Ettinghausen, 1972, no. 25.

60

60 Medallion carpet

incomplete

North-west or central Persia, 16th century
L. 369 cm. W. 247 cm.
Paris, Collections of the Mobilier National, no. GOB 1375

Bequeathed to the Mobilier National by Elie Delaunay in 1892, this splendidly decorative carpet has been very much shortened and must originally have had the long narrow format commonly seen in carpets attributed to north-west Persia; the field is complete in the width, but the main border is missing all round. The warp and weft, as well as the pile, are of wool. The great star-medallion of sixteen points has a cloud-like rim and a mainly orange-red ground with flowers and arabesques; a large cartouche and finial project from it at either end and there are small finials on the diagonal axes. The yellow field is covered with a large repeating pattern consisting of a very complex mesh of coiling floral stems, arabesques and cloud-bands, on three different levels, animated by the presence of small birds; it is a pity that the loss of the ends of the carpet deprives us of the pleasure of seeing the full development of this pattern. There is an elegant minor border of arabesques and flowers on a blue ground. This carpet seems to exemplify a refined metropolitan design, of which a carpet such as no. 58 is a somewhat simplified, more vigorous and perhaps more provincial version. Tabriz and Kashan have been suggested as possible places of origin.

Literature
Pope, 1939, pl. 1115; Erdmann, 1955, p. 33.

61 Cartouche carpet

North-west or central Persia, 16th century
L. 800 cm. W. 400 cm.
Lyon, Musée Historique des Tissus, no. 25.423

Though much damaged and patched, this carpet still remains one of the great carpets of the world. Its large size allows ample space for the deployment of the unusual pattern, whereas its fellow in the Metropolitan Museum of Art, New York, although in much better condition, shows the pattern in a somewhat reduced form.
Designs of this type, composed of variously shaped compartments or cartouches, had long been employed in architectural decoration and in the arts of the book; in carpets, their earliest recorded appearance is an example in a miniature of Bihzad, dated 1487/8. The design of the present carpet is composed of dark blue octofoils containing a Chinese dragon-and-phoenix, dark brown octofoils containing four Chinese lion *ch'i-lins*, and palmette-shaped cartouches in green and tomato-red containing either interlaced arabesques or a pair of flying geese; the intervening sections of ivory ground show Chinese cloud-bands and coiling floral stems. The basic idea of medallions with radiating cartouches is related to that of the more or less contemporary Ardabil and Chelsea carpets (figs. 32, 33), though here the octofoil medallions do not dominate, but are integrated into a repeating pattern. This pattern can be read in a tantalizing variety of ways. One can see eight cartouches radiating from the dragon octofoil and none from the lion octofoil, or four radiating from each; one can see the pattern as ranks and files of free-standing motifs, or as a grid of horizontals and verticals, or as an enormous diagonal lattice. There is a teasing playfulness about the concept of these cartouche carpets which is quite different from the majestic solemnity of the Ardabil carpets or the courtly elegance of the Chelsea carpet, notwithstanding their similarities. This gives an idea of the wide range of the designs which the court painters supplied to the carpet workshops at this period. Kurt Erdmann and others have claimed these cartouche carpets for the workshops of Tabriz; Charles Grant Ellis suggests Kashan or Qazvin as possible places of origin. A much simplified version of this field pattern is found in a group of north-west Persian medallion carpets, in the Vienna collection and elsewhere.

The border pattern of the present carpet consists of superb dark blue cartouches with cloud-bands and flowers, alternating with octofoils with another version of the dragon-and-phoenix motif, all on a tomato-red ground with more flying geese and flowers. The broad yellow guard stripes show flowers, cloud-bands and arabesques. Despite the great size of the carpet, the whole design is executed with something approaching the scale and precision of miniature painting.

Literature
Cox, 1900, pl. LVIII; Erdmann, 1950, no. 100; Erdmann, 1955, p. 31; Ellis, 1965, pp. 52–3; Dimand, 1973, no. 6.

61

62

62 The Anhalt medallion carpet

North-west Persia, second half 16th century
L. 808 cm. w. 414 cm.
New York, The Metropolitan Museum of Art, no. 46.128;
Gift of Samuel H. Kress Foundation, 1946

This amazing carpet, in virtually new condition, was
formerly in the collection of the Dukes of Anhalt at their
castle at Dessau, where it is said to have lain in a loft,
forgotten, until the middle of the 19th century. It is
claimed that it was part of the booty taken from the Turks
at Vienna in 1683, but this could well be a tradition of
comparatively recent date. Finely executed in woollen pile
on a cotton warp and silk weft, it is in a style which has
much in common with the finest carpets of the first half or
middle of the 16th century, such as the Ardabil and Chelsea
carpets (figs. 32, 33) or the cartouche carpet, no. 61.

Stuart Cary Welch, in a letter to the compiler, has
suggested an affinity between the arabesques in the carpet
and the 'fine round hand' of Mir Musavvir, one of Shah
Tahmasp's major artists, active in the second quarter of
the 16th century. Despite the fineness and precision of the
execution the carpet suffers, in comparison with the other
carpets mentioned, from a degree of monotony in the
ornament and certain harshness in drawing and colour.
Some of the best qualified carpet specialists have
expressed misgivings, orally, as to whether it can have
been made as early as the style might suggest. There can
be no doubt, however, that this is one of the stars of the
marvellous collection of carpets in the Metropolitan
Museum of Art and we are most grateful to the Museum
authorities for allowing it to return to London, where it
was first exhibited to the public more than half a century
ago, in the great exhibition of Persian art in 1931.

The large red medallion in the centre, with a design of

88

flowers, arabesques and cloud-bands, has twenty lobes, a form which seems to have become fashionable in the second half of the 16th century. From it, at either end, project a large blue cartouche and a red finial, with similar patterns. The yellow field is overspread with a dense mesh of coiling stems, arabesques and cloud-bands on three levels, somewhat reminiscent of that of the Paris medallion carpet, no. 60, but whereas that is a repeating pattern on which the medallion is superimposed, the field pattern of the Anhalt carpet, like other artist-designed carpets, is freely drawn and carefully related to the medallion, cartouches and finials. Among the scrolls are a dozen peacocks with extremely colourful plumage. The red border shows large, thin arabesque scrolls, cloud-bands and flowers; similar ornaments appear in the guard stripes.

The carpet is generally attributed to Tabriz.

Literature
Pope, 1939, pls. 1137–9; Bode & Kühnel, 1955, p. 84; Erdmann, 1955, fig. 66; Dimand, 1973, no. 7.

63 Medallion carpet

fragments

North-west or east Persia, second half 16th century
L. 165 cm. W. 100 cm.
New York, The Brooklyn Museum, no. 36.213 a-g;
Presented to The Brooklyn Museum in memory of Florence Gibb Pratt, April 24, 1936, by Herbert L. Pratt

Formerly with Stefano Bardini in Florence, this group of fragments passed to the Yerkes Collection and thence to Herbert L. Pratt, who gave them to the Brooklyn Museum. They have a silk warp and weft and a woollen pile. The border fragments with compartments containing Chinese *ch'i-lins*, birds and arabesques are of a type associated with carpets from Herat, the great artistic centre of eastern Persia, now in Afghanistan. These and the fragmentary guard stripe with cloud-bands apparently belong to the same carpet as some larger fragments which formerly belonged to Baron Hatvany in Budapest; the latter include part of a unique central medallion depicting a courtly scene with many figures, in the style of Persian miniature painting, and a section of the field design, with trees, animals and birds, all treated in a naturalistic style (Pope, 1939, pl. 1141). The complete design must have been related to those of a large carpet divided between Cracow and Paris, and others in Los Angeles, Berlin and the Schwarzenberg Collection. It is tempting to suppose that the Brooklyn fragments with birds and trees and the section of a corner medallion with four winged figures, the houris who minister to the blessed in Paradise, may also be from the Hatvany carpet. Erdmann considers this to be probable and envisages an important carpet, over 7 metres long, specially commissioned from the workshops of Tabriz or Qazvin. Charles Grant Ellis, on the other hand, considers that the Brooklyn fragments come from more than one carpet and proposes an attribution to Herat.

Literature
Mumford, 1910, pl. VII; Ellis, 1965, p. 47 ff.; Erdmann, 1970, pp. 74, 176.

63

64 Medallion and animal carpet

Central Persia, possibly Kerman, late 16th or early 17th century
L. 509 cm. W. 275 cm.
Lugano, Switzerland, Thyssen-Bornemisza Collection, no. 669a

Formerly in the collections of Comtesse de Béhague and the Marquis de Ganay, Paris, this is a good example of a small group of medallion carpets in a characteristic and easily recognizable style. These have become known as Sanguszko carpets, after a splendid example belonging to Prince Roman Sanguszko which is said to have been captured at the battle of Chocim in 1621 (currently exhibited at the Metropolitan Museum of Art, New York). The sixteen-lobed red medallion has interlacing strapwork arabesques, with four flying ducks at the centre; from it, at either end, project palmettes, cartouches, and finials containing pairs of peacocks. The ivory field is covered with a design of coiling floral stems, enlivened with birds and numerous mythical and natural animals, singly or in combat. Between yellow and ivory floral guard stripes, the red border shows animal combats in leaf-shaped medallions, alternating with combats of phoenix and *ch'i-lin* among clouds. According to Professor Cammann's interpretation of the symbolism of the carpet, the border represents the 'Sky Door', the field the 'Celestial Eden', the central medallion the 'Sun Gate' leading to the highest Heaven, while the ducks symbolize the Divine Presence.

Another Sanguszko carpet with a comparable design, in the Victoria and Albert Museum, London, has corner-medallions with winged genii, as in no. 63.

The Sanguszko carpets have been variously attributed in the past to Kashan, Kerman, Qazvin and Yazd. Jenny Housego has pointed out notable similarities of style and motifs in the tile mosaics of the Ganj 'Ali Khan Caravanserai at Kerman, about 1598. Technically, Sanguszko carpets like this one, with a cotton warp, a silk and wool weft, and a woollen pile, resemble the vase carpets, which are often ascribed to Kerman, but there is no obvious stylistic relationship between the two groups. There is general agreement that the Sanguszko carpets were made about the time of Shah Abbas (reigned 1587–1629).

Literature
Pope, 1939, pl. 1210; Beattie, 1972, p. 27; Cammann, 1975, pp. 251–3; Beattie, 1976, no. 2; Beattie, Housego & Morton, 1977, p. 464 ff.

64

Silk pile carpets

During the 16th century a number of supremely luxurious carpets were made for palace use, with the pile very finely knotted in silk instead of in wool. The great silk Mamluk carpet from the Imperial Collection in Vienna is a unique example from the carpet-making areas of the eastern Mediterranean. Three sumptuous Persian medallion carpets of this kind have survived in Europe, all depicting hunters pursuing wild animals, and all with the silk pile further enriched with areas of brocading in gold and silver thread. The largest and most elaborate of these formed part of the Imperial Collection in Vienna; another, from a princely collection in Italy, is now in the Museum of Fine Arts, Boston; the third, in the Swedish Royal Collections, we are privileged to include in the present exhibition by gracious permission of His Majesty the King of Sweden (no. 65). A fourth large Persian medallion carpet of the 16th century, knotted in silk but without brocading, seems unfortunately to have disappeared in Poland during the last war; it was reputed to have been part of the booty taken from the Turks at Vienna in 1683. In addition, a number of small Persian rugs, with silk pile but without brocading, have survived from the 16th century; about ten of these have medallion designs, generally with flowers (nos. 67, 68), while another four show animals in a landscape (no. 66). These silk rugs are exquisitely designed and executed. The colours produced by the silk-dyers are ravishingly beautiful and the changing hues, as one moves from one end of the rug to the other and sees the light reflected at different angles from the silk pile, give an enchanting variety of effect. All these carpets and rugs seem to be very closely interrelated in design and colour and presumably all were made in the same centre. This is generally believed to have been Kashan, which is known to have produced other work in silk and metal thread (no. 73).

In 1597/98 Shah Abbas (reigned 1587–1629) transferred his capital from Qazvin to Isfahan, which he began to develop on a grand scale. Among other things he set up state manufactories there, which evidently included carpet workshops. Isfahan soon became a great cosmopolitan city and more than one European visitor in the 17th century remarked on the sumptuous gold and silk carpets to be seen there. A silk and gold carpet in the form of a church vestment, in the Victoria and Albert Museum, London, may well have been commissioned for one of the Christian churches of Isfahan. The numerous Persian carpets with silk pile, often brocaded with gold, which have survived from the 17th century – estimated at around four hundred – are generally attributed to Isfahan or Kashan. Examples in Venice and Copenhagen are believed to have been brought as gifts by Persian ambassadors in 1603, 1622 and 1639. Many more no doubt arrived in Europe by way of trade. The Coronation Carpet of the Danish Royal House was a gift from the Dutch East India Company in 1662. These carpets, which invariably have floral designs, are less finely knotted and less well dyed than their 16th century predecessors and many now look rather faded and sad. But when new, with bright colours and glittering with gold, they must have been very striking and they evidently became an indispensable element of interior decoration in the great Baroque houses of Europe. Though undoubtedly Persian, these 17th century silk carpets are commonly described as Polonaise or Polish, owing to an erroneous identification of the coat of arms on one example, more than a century ago (no. 69); the name is obviously wrong, but is retained as a useful label for classification purposes. An alternative name, Shah Abbas carpets, is sometimes used, but is apt to be even more misleading. Besides a considerable number of large carpets, the group includes many small rugs, which were no doubt used in Europe mainly as table-carpets (no. 70).

Literature
Pope, 1939, pp. 2335–47, 2388–2401; Bode & Kühnel, 1955, pp. 87–90, 140–7; Erdmann, 1955, pp. 34, 40–1; Erdmann, 1970, pp. 61–5; Dimand, 1973, pp. 54–65.

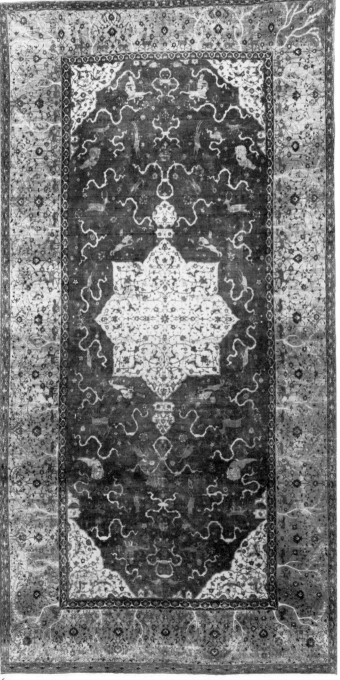

65

65 The Swedish Royal hunting carpet

Persia, possibly Kashan, late 16th century
L. 555 cm. W. 285 cm.
Stockholm, The Royal Collections, no. 467
REPRODUCED IN COLOUR PAGE 43

The silk hunting carpet in the Royal Palace in Stockholm is one of the great carpets of the world. We are deeply indebted to His Majesty the King of Sweden for giving his consent to its inclusion in the present exhibition, the first occasion on which it has been shown outside Sweden.

It is one of three silk hunting carpets – so-called because the design depicts a hunt of wild beasts – which survived from the great age of Persian carpet weaving in European collections. The largest and most elaborate of the three is that from the former Imperial Collection, now in the Österreichisches Museum für angewandte Kunst in Vienna. The smallest, formerly belonging to the Marchese Torrigiani in Italy and now in the Museum of Fine Arts in Boston, is a reduced version of the Vienna example; both show a mêlée of mounted huntsmen in the field, dragons and phoenixes in the central and corner medallions, and groups of seated figures in the main borders. The Stockholm carpet is similar to these two in its technique, with silk warp and weft and silk pile interspersed with areas brocaded with metal thread, and in its design of hunters wearing the characteristic stick-turban of 16th century Persia. Yet there are also many differences, all tending towards greater openness and simplicity in the design, which, in conjunction with the rather better preservation of the colours of the silk pile in this piece, makes it in some respects the most impressive and certainly the most easily comprehended of the three.

The eight-pointed star-medallion at the centre, with cartouches and finials projecting above and below, and the quarter-medallions in the corners, with cartouches and finials projecting from the cardinal points, show delicate linear patterns of floral stems and arabesques on a background of silver or light gold thread. On the rich purplish-red field a dozen hunters, unmounted and unarmed, wrestle heroically with lions, while other animals run and prowl among sparse floral scrolls and large cloud-bands in gold or silver thread. In the main border small animals and birds are seen among floral scrolls and flowering trees, like those in the border of the Boston carpet. The guard stripes have elegant patterns of arabesques and flowers. The design of the whole, though relatively simple and direct, is conceived with supreme elegance and discretion which, coupled with the deep and glowing colours of the silk and the sheen of the metal, make this one of the most sumptuous experiences in the world of Oriental carpets.

Like most silk carpets of its period it is generally attributed to Kashan. It is believed to be rather later than the other two silk hunting carpets, perhaps from the end of the 16th century. F. R. Martin conjectured that it might have reached Sweden through the marriage of King Charles X Gustaf to Hedwig Eleonora, Princess of Gottorp, and that it was among the gifts sent by the Shah of Persia to Duke Friedrich III of Gottorp in 1639.

Literature
Martin, 1908, pp. 54–6, pls. IV, V; Pope, 1939, pls. 1193, 1194; Erdmann, 1970, p. 73.

66

This all-silk rug, of the usual beautiful quality associated with the silk rugs of Kashan, was given to the Metropolitan Museum of Art by Mrs. Douglas M. Moffat. On a red field with flowers and palmettes, it has a dark blue eight-pointed star-medallion in the centre, with a cartouche and finial at either end, and similar light tan quarter-medallions in the corners, all with floral designs. More flowers and palmettes appear in the green border and in the guard stripes. Another silk rug with a closely related design belongs to the Portuguese-Israelite Community in Amsterdam.

Literature
Erdmann, 1970, p. 62 ff.; Dimand, 1973, no. 16.

67

66 Silk animal rug

Persia, possibly Kashan, second half 16th century
L. 124 cm. W. 109 cm.
Paris, Musée du Louvre, no. 6741; Islamic Section

Besides the large carpets with hunting scenes (no. 65), other silk medallion carpets, of comparable quality but without metal thread, have designs of animals. A large example formerly preserved in Poland unfortunately disappeared during the last war, but a smaller example still survives in the Gulbenkian Foundation, Lisbon. In addition, a group of four small silk rugs are designed without medallions, but with scenes of animals in a landscape, to be viewed like a picture, with no reversal of the pattern. Besides the present piece, which was given to the Louvre by Joanny Peytel, three other and rather larger examples are in museums in Detroit, New York and Tehran. All four make use of parts of the same cartoon and show the exquisite quality of design and colour which is characteristic of the 16th century silk rugs ascribed to Kashan. This one has a blue field with mythical and natural animals, singly and in combat, in a landscape of flowering plants. Between ivory guard stripes with floral designs, the red border shows lion masks in lotus palmettes, as in the border of the Vienna hunting carpet, alternating with oddly shaped flowers, which are evidently abbreviated versions of those in the border of no. 67.

Literature
Sarre & Trenkwald, 1929, pl. 40; Erdmann, 1970, p. 62 ff.; Beattie, 1976, no. 5.

67 Silk medallion rug

Persia, possibly Kashan, second half 16th century
L. 251 cm. W. 168 cm.
New York, The Metropolitan Museum of Art, no. 58.46;
Gift of Mrs. Douglas M. Moffat, 1958

68 Silk medallion rug

Persia, possibly Kashan, second half 16th century
L. 245 cm. W. 185 cm.
Paris, Collections of the Mobilier National, no. GOB 1354

Bequeathed by Albert Goupil to the Mobilier National, this is perhaps the most beautiful of the small silk medallion rugs of Kashan. The red field has a pattern of floral stems and cloud-scrolls. The finely drawn green quatrefoil medallion in the centre and the ivory quarter-medallions in the corners have patterns of arabesques and flowers, and finials projecting from the cardinal points. Opulent patterns of flowers and palmettes fill the yellow border and the guard stripes. The rug is a masterpiece of

68

In this case the field of the carpet is patterned with two interlaced systems of arabesques, intersecting with floral scrolls bearing long curving leaves, blossoms and palmettes. These ornaments pass without interruption into the lozenge-shaped medallion which encloses a shield at the centre of the carpet; similar shields appear in the four corners. The shields are blazoned with a cross and four birds, are surrounded with elaborate mantling, and surmounted by a crest of a camel's head issuing from a crown; the design for these must have been supplied by the European client who commissioned the carpet, but the arms remain unidentified. The border, on a ground of silver thread, shows flowers and palmettes between pairs of very long curving leaves. The warp of the carpet is of cotton, the weft and the pile of silk.

Literature
Mańkowski, 1954; Erdmann, 1970, p. 206; Dimand, 1973, no. 17.

Persian floral design, rendered in exquisite colours and knotted with sensitive precision. Another silk rug with a related design is in the Metropolitan Museum of Art, New York.

Literature
Sarre & Trenkwald, 1929, pls. 41, 42; Pope, 1939, pl. 1201; Erdmann, 1970, p. 61 ff.

69 Silk Polonaise carpet

Persia, possibly Isfahan, first half 17th century
L. 483 cm. w. 215 cm.
New York, The Metropolitan Museum of Art, no. 45.106;
Gift of John D. Rockefeller, Jr., 1945

Formerly in the family collection of Prince Czartoryski, this remarkable carpet was given to the Metropolitan Museum of Art by John D. Rockefeller, Jr. When it was shown in the Paris exhibition of 1878 it was mistakenly assumed that the five heraldic shields which appear on it must be those of the Czartoryski and the erroneous conclusion was drawn that this and similar carpets were made in Poland. It soon became clear that they were of Persian manufacture, but the term Polonaise or Polish has remained as a useful label for a large class of carpets with silk pile and often with brocading in metal thread, which were evidently exported to Europe in considerable numbers during the 17th century and became indispensable furnishings for the palaces and great houses of the Baroque period.

70 Silk Polonaise rug

Persia, possibly Isfahan, 17th century
L. 208 cm. W. 122 cm.
His Grace The Duke of Buccleuch and Queensberry, K.T.,
Boughton no. 9

A characteristic example of the small Polonaise rugs, this
one has a cotton warp and weft, silk pile and extensive
remains of brocading in gold and silver thread. Quatrefoils
in the centre and corners still hint at the old medallion-
and-corner designs, but this is really an infinitely
extensible repeating pattern, with coloured bands defining
compartments of various shapes, and curving floral stems
flowing easily from one compartment to the next. This
type of pattern was evidently popular; there are related
examples in the Palazzo Pitti, in the Residenzmuseum in
Munich from the Wittelbach family collection, and in
several other collections. The border pattern includes
arabesques and palmettes, between floral guard stripes.

Literature
Erdmann, 1950, no. 89; Beattie, 1976, no. 5a.

70

Silk tapestry carpets

A group of between twenty and thirty Persian rugs from the
late 16th and 17th centuries are executed in silk and in gold
and silver thread, not in the carpet-knotting technique, but
in flat-woven tapestry. The principal example of this class is
a fairly large carpet in the Residenzmuseum, Munich, which
has a medallion-and-corner design with hunting and other
figure subjects, very much in the manner of the great
hunting carpets with silk pile, which are attributed to Kashan.
Some of the smaller examples also have medallion or cartouche
designs with animals and figures (nos. 71, 72). Others have
floral designs. Among them are some which incorporate an
heraldic shield with the arms of the Vasa Kings of Poland
(no. 73) and it seems very likely that these were some of the
carpets with the royal arms which are known, from documentary evidence, to have been woven in Kashan for the
Polish King in 1601–2. For this reason it is customary to
attribute most of the silk tapestry rugs to Kashan, though
Isfahan has been suggested as a possible origin for some.
Because of the Polish connection such rugs have sometimes
been called Polish or Polonaise, but it seems less confusing
to reserve this term for silk pile carpets of the 17th century.
With their attractive designs, rendered in bright colours and
glittering with precious metal, these tapestry rugs were
evidently welcomed in Europe just as the silk pile carpets
were (fig.13). Examples have also survived in the religious
shrines of Persia and at least one example travelled as far
east as Japan.

Literature
Pope, 1939, pp. 2401–6; Spuhler, 1978; Dimand, 1973, pp. 65–7.

71 Silk tapestry rug

Persia, possibly Kashan, late 16th century
L. 192 cm. W. 125 cm.
Lugano, Switzerland, Thyssen-Bornemisza Collection, no. 669

Formerly in the Figdor Collection in Vienna, this famous
and much-published rug is a good example of this class,
woven in the tapestry technique with gold and silver
thread and brightly coloured silks, now somewhat faded.
The design is of the cartouche or compartment type,
composed of rows of cartouches in quatrefoil, oblong and
palmette-shaped forms. These, and the sections of ivory
ground between them, are occupied by lion masks,
dragons, a phoenix and other mythical or natural animals
and birds, singly or in combat. The sky-blue border has
arabesques, and oblong cartouches containing birds,
between red and orange guard stripes with floral
cartouches. Professor Cammann interprets the whole
design as a view of Paradise beyond the Sky. Only two
other silk tapestry rugs with this type of design are known.
One, in the Wher Collection, is currently exhibited in the
Carpet Study Room of the Victoria and Albert Museum,
London (illustrated in Bennett, 1977, p. 86). The other, in
Japan, is reputed to have been the favourite campaigning
coat of the great Japanese general Hideyoshi (1536–98).
These rugs are generally attributed to Kashan.

Literature
Pope, 1939, p. 2404, pl. 1268A; Beattie, 1972, p. 31 ff.; Cammann, 1975,
pp.253–5; Beattie, 1976, no. 8.

71

72 Silk tapestry rug

Persia, possibly Kashan, late 16th or early 17th century
L. 249 cm. W. 139 cm.
Paris, Musée du Louvre, no. 5946; Islamic Section

Given to the Louvre by Monsieur Doistau in 1904, this rug in silk and metal thread tapestry has a medallion-and-corner design. The yellowish pointed oval central medallion, with twenty lobes, and with cartouches and finials at either end, shows Bahram Gur, on horseback, encountering the dragon, an episode from Firdawsi's *Shah Namah* or Book of Kings. The quarter-medallions in the corners illustrate the story of the lovers Laylah and Majnun. The blue field of the rug has a design of animals, singly or in combat, and the borders show heavy floral arabesques and palmettes. The rug is often attributed to Kashan, though M. S. Dimand has suggested Isfahan. It is rather closely related to the Figdor rug (no. 71); the guard stripes are the same and the border pattern and the animals are similar, though the present piece is a little coarser and possibly later. It is hard to resist the conclusion that the designers and weavers of these rugs set out to create something that was not only luxurious, but also amusing. Surely the little scene in the corners – the scampering rabbit and the odd little creature holding the rein of Laylah's very shaggy camel, with its towering howdah – was always intended to be comic.

Literature
Pope, 1939, p. 2405, pl. 1262; Beattie, 1976, no. 6.

72

73 Silk tapestry rug

Persia, Kashan, 1601–2
L. 238 cm. W. 132 cm.
Munich, Bayerische Verwaltung der Staatlichen Schlösser, Gärten und Seen, Residenzmuseum, no. WC3
REPRODUCED IN COLOUR PAGE 44

This silk rug has a floral and medallion design of a common Persian type, but in place of the central medallion a rectangular panel has been woven, containing a shield with the arms of the Vasa Kings of Poland. The rug is believed to have come to the Wittelsbach family as part of the dowry of the Polish princess Anna Catharina Constanza, who married the Elector Philipp Wilhelm von der Pfalz in 1642; another rug of the same kind remains in the Wittelsbach family collection and part of a third is in the Textile Museum, Washington, D.C. It is likely that these rugs are referred to in a document preserved in the archives at Warsaw. This indicates that in 1601 an Armenian, Sefer Muratowicz, was sent by King Sigismund III to Kashan and that on 12th September 1602 he presented an account to the Polish Treasury as follows:

Price of the objects which I bought in Persia in the
city of Kashan for his Majesty our gracious King
2 *pairs of carpets at* 40 *crowns, together* — 160 *crowns*
2 *carpets at* 41 *crowns, together* — 82 *crowns*
For the execution of the royal arms extra — 5 *crowns*
2 *carpets at* 39 *crowns, together* — 78 *crowns*

Though it cannot be absolutely proved that the extant
rugs are the ones mentioned in the document, this does
seem a very strong possibility. In any event, both the
document and the rugs provide a graphic proof that, at the
beginning of the 17th century, it was possible for
European clients to order specially designed rugs direct
from the carpet workshops in Persia.

Literature
Mańkowski, 1936; Pope, 1939, pl. 1268B; Erdmann, 1970, p. 205 ff.

73

Animal and palmette carpets

Wild animals and animal combats are ancient symbols of
temporal authority and power. Professor Cammann, taking
a different view, suggests that they may also be symbols of
man's spiritual struggles. Designs with animals, singly or in
combat, have already been seen in Persian medallion and
cartouche carpets, in wool and in silk. Animal motifs also
occur in a number of Persian carpets in wool, in conjunction
with all-over patterns of coiling floral stems, large palmettes
and cloud-bands. These animal carpets are often of quite
large size, especially the pair in Vienna and New York which
are said to have been given to Leopold I of Austria by Peter
the Great of Russia in 1698. Such carpets were certainly
imported to western Europe long before that date, as can be
seen from various paintings, such as the portraits of the Earl
and Countess of Arundel painted by Daniel Mytens in or
before 1618. Probably they were made in a number of
centres, but most of the surviving pieces are attributed to
eastern Persia and particularly to Herat (no. 74). Others
were made in Mughal India (nos. 76, 77) whence they were
exported, for example, to Portugal and England. A Mughal
piece in the National Gallery of Art, Washington, D.C., was
formerly at Belvoir Castle. A very large example, formerly at
Knole and now in the Metropolitan Museum of Art, New
York, and another in the Victoria and Albert Museum,
London, specially commissioned, with the arms of Fremlin
(fig. 36), show the animals in landscape settings with trees.

Many other carpets were made with all-over designs of
coiling floral stems, palmettes and cloud-bands similar to
those of the animal carpets, but with the animate presence
reduced to a few birds (no. 75), or more often eliminated
altogether. Carpets of this kind were evidently exported to
Europe in very large numbers and they are seen in many
Dutch, Flemish, Spanish and other European paintings of
the 17th century (fig. 24). No doubt these carpets, too, were
made in a number of different centres. It used to be customary
to attribute many of them to Isfahan, but nowadays they are
generally attributed to east Persia, particularly to Herat.
Related designs were also woven in Mughal India, for
example the splendid armorial carpet woven at Lahore in
1631–2 for Robert Bell and now displayed in the Hall of
the Girdlers' Company in London (fig. 35). A considerable
number of carpets with designs of this class have been found
in Portugal and it seems likely that most of these, and many
others formerly attributed to Persia, may in fact have been
export pieces from Mughal India. Similar examples are still
to be found in English country houses such as Boughton and
Knole, though the grandest of the Knole pieces is now in
the Metropolitan Museum of Art.

Literature
Pope, 1939, pp. 2358–70; Bode & Kühnel, 1955, pp. 107–15; Erdmann,
1955, pp. 37–9; Dimand, 1973, pp. 53–4, 67–72, 85–6.

74

75

74 Animal carpet

fragment

East Persia, possibly Herat, late 16th or early 17th century
L. 184 cm. W. 126 cm.
Vienna, Österreichisches Museum für angewandte Kunst,
no. Or 311

This particularly well-preserved fragment gives an excellent
idea of the high quality of design, colour and execution
found in animal carpets of the Herat style. It represents
about one eighth of the complete carpet, roughly a quarter
of the length and just under half the width. The warp and
weft are of silk and the pile of wool. On the red ground
mythical and natural animals appear among floral scrolls,
palmettes and cloud-bands. The ivory border has a most
impressive and stately pattern of arabesques, palmettes,
flowers and cloud-bands, and there are elegant guard
stripes. Other carpets of very similar design, both in the
field and border, are in Vienna – from the former Imperial
Collection – and the Victoria and Albert Museum,
London.

Literature
Sarre & Trenkwald, 1926, pl. 10.

75 Coiling stem and palmette carpet

fragment

Persia or India, late 16th or early 17th century
L. 196 cm. W. 180 cm.
London, Victoria and Albert Museum, no. 721–1884

Formerly in the Castellani Collection in Italy, this
fragment, representing exactly half a carpet, was acquired
by the Victoria and Albert Museum in 1884. It is a good
and probably early example of the designs with coiling
floral stems, large palmettes and cloud-bands, but without
animate life except occasionally, as in this piece, a few
birds. This type of design is seen in carpets depicted in
innumerable 17th century paintings, by Rubens, van Dyck,
Velasquez, Vermeer and many other European artists
(fig. 24). Hundreds of carpets with such designs have been
found in Portugal and other western European countries;
examples can still be seen on the floors of great English
country houses such as Knole and Boughton. This piece
has a silk warp, a cotton weft and a woollen pile with some
cotton; it is an unusually luxurious example, with a good
deal of brocading in gold and silver thread, now much
worn. The border, like the field, has flowers and palmettes,
and there are floral guard stripes. Carpets of this class
were at one time often attributed to Isfahan. Now they are
generally attributed to east Persia, particularly Herat. But
there is a strong possibility that many of them were made
in India. The question of their provenance requires
further research.

Literature
Erdmann, 1955, fig. 79.

76

76 Animal carpet

India, Mughal empire, first half 17th century
L. 604 cm. W. 244 cm.
Private Collection

Formerly in the collection of the Earls of Ilchester, this carpet was long regarded as Persian and, indeed, the design of mythical and natural animals, depicted singly and in combat among coiling floral stems and palmettes, is closely related to those of the carpets attributed to Herat. The colouring, however, and many details of the design are characteristic of the carpet workshops which had been set up in India – no doubt staffed initially by Persian craftsmen – under the patronage of the Mughal Emperor Akbar (1556–1605). The carpet has a cotton warp and weft and a woollen pile. As in the carpets showing animals in landscape settings (no. 66), the animal design here, on a

dark blue field, is intended to be viewed from one end of the carpet. The unit of design occupies the full width of the field and is about 2.5 metres long; at each repetition in the length it is reversed from left to right, as in the Mughal animal carpet from Knole now in the Metropolitan Museum of Art, New York. The proportions of the carpet might suggest the possibility of use on a long table, like the Girdlers' carpet (fig. 35), but in fact it was clearly intended for use on the floor, as the red border with its unusual pattern of animals and flowers is designed for viewing from within the field of the carpet, and would be upside-down if it hung over the edges of a table.

Literature
Kendrick & Tattersall, 1922, pp. 20, 104, pl. 12; Beattie, 1964, no. 36.

77 Animal carpet

India, Mughal empire, first half 17th century
L. 768 cm. W. 296 cm.
Berlin, Staatliche Museen Preussischer Kulturbesitz,
Museum für Islamische Kunst, no. I.6/74

This imposing carpet has many points in common with no. 76. On the ivory ground there are, as before, mythical and natural animals, singly or in combat, among coiling floral stems and palmettes; here, however, the animals are somewhat less important, whereas the floral ornament has become more complex. The unit of design occupies the full width of the field and is about 1.75 metres long, repeating four times in the length of the field, with each repeat inverted in relation to its predecessor. This means that the best view of the design is offered, not to a viewer looking along the length of the carpet as with no. 76, but to one looking across the carpet at the mid-point in the length. Professor Brisch, who has made a very thorough analysis of the layout of the carpet (see diagrams, where A and B represent apparent sections of the design, each centred on a palmette, while C and D represent the real unit of design and its mirror-image), suggests that it may have been designed to lie transversely in front of a throne, perhaps the throne of Shah Jahan himself (1628–58). The border shows a green floral trail with leaf-shaped cartouches containing lotus-blossoms and flower vases, on a red ground with a small floral pattern in pink. The carpet has a cotton warp and weft and a woollen pile.

Literature
Berlin, 1979, no. 678.

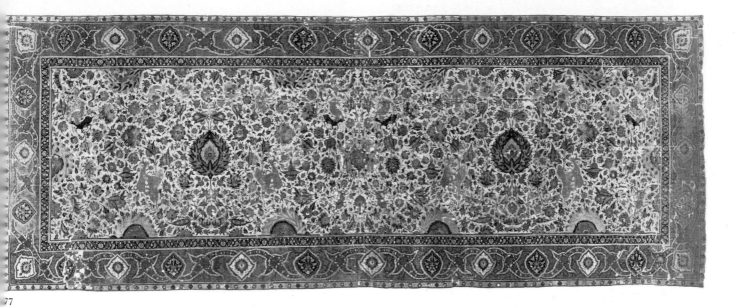

77

Vase carpets and others related

The numerous group of vase carpets take their name from the vases which figure fairly inconspicuously in their designs (nos. 78, 79). The main feature of the carpets is a riot of fantastic blossoms, infinitely varied, and many of them of giant size. These large flowers are arranged on wavy stems which intersect, often on three different levels, to form huge curvilinear lattice patterns. Around the large blossoms coil thinner stems with smaller flowers and curving leaves. The whole effect is one of astonishing floral profusion. The standard of design, dyeing and execution is very high. The technique and materials are characteristic, with a cotton warp, and with three passes of weft between the rows of knots, the first and third being of wool and the second of silk or cotton. This particular combination has become known as vase-technique and is found in carpets of other designs such as the Sanguszko medallion carpets (no. 64). There are good reasons for believing that this technique was employed at Kerman and the surrounding area, and vase carpets are generally attributed to Kerman. It is interesting that a tile panel in the Friday Mosque at Kerman has a three-plane lattice pattern with similar flowers. The vase design probably originated during the reign of Shah Abbas (1587–1629) and continued to be woven throughout the 17th century and beyond. These carpets are depicted only rarely in European paintings, but some representatives of this large class certainly reached Europe during the 17th century (fig. 25); no. 79 may well have been in a Polish church collection since that time. In a later period, a fine carpet of this type hung in the dining room of the English poet and designer William Morris (now in the Victoria and Albert Museum, London) and it is not difficult to recognize an affinity between these tangled thickets of flowers and the enchanted gardens of 19th century art.

Besides the vase designs, a number of variant and more or less related designs were produced, probably in the same area and at the same period. Among these the sickle-leaf designs are particularly striking and full of movement (no. 80).

Vase designs do not seem to have been widely imitated, but the exhibition includes an astonishing palace carpet from Mughal India which shows a vase design magnified to a gigantic size (no. 81).

Literature
Pope, 1939, pp. 2372–88; Bode & Kühnel, 1955, pp. 123–31; Erdmann, 1955, pp. 34–8; Dimand, 1973, pp. 72–7; Beattie, 1976; Beattie, Housego & Morton, 1977.

78

78 Vase carpet

fragment

Persia, possibly Kerman, early 17th century
L. 245 cm. W. 144 cm.
Berlin, Staatliche Museen Preussischer Kulturbesitz,
Museum für Islamische Kunst, no. I.8/72
REPRODUCED IN COLOUR PAGE 45

Formerly in the collection of Friedrich Sarre, this famous
and much-admired fragment was acquired by the Museum
für Islamische Kunst, Berlin, in 1972. It represents rather
more than one quarter of a carpet which originally
measured about 5 metres by 2.5 metres; other fragments
of the same carpet are in museums in Cairo, London and
Washington, D.C. The carpet appears to be the earliest
extant version of the vase design and shows it in the full
beauty of the original conception. A very large pattern
unit occupies half the width of the dark blue field and its
entire length (most of the upper part is seen in the
Washington fragment). The right half of the field,
partially visible near the right edge of this fragment, shows
the same design in reverse, but the colours are varied so
that none of the blossoms exactly repeat their counterparts
on the opposite side; in fact not one of the many scores of
large blossoms in the carpet is exactly like another. The
carpet ensnares the beholder in an enchanted garden of
fantastic flowers, which at first sight seem to flourish in
wild abandon, but are actually disciplined by a strict,
though unobtrusive, system. All the large blossoms and
the vases are carried on, and oriented by, sinuous stems
which, half-hidden among the flowers and among other,
thinner coiling stems, form three intersecting curvilinear
lattices, one red, one ivory and one blue, on three different
levels. The restless movement of the swelling wind-tossed
blossoms among which only the vases offer moments of
stability and repose, corresponded to a taste in design
which was widespread in the 17th century. Designs of
related character are found in Indian painted cottons, in
Turkish and European woven silks and in English crewel-
work embroidery. The delicate floral border and its very
narrow plain guard stripes are typical of the earliest vase
carpets. Both the field and border pattern of this carpet
recur, in stiffer versions, in many later pieces.

Literature
Ellis, 1968, p. 19; Ellis, 1975, p. 26; Beattie, 1976, nos. 33–5; Berlin,
1979, no. 677.

79 Vase carpet

Persia, possibly Kerman, second half 17th century
L. 269 cm. W. 174 cm.
Lugano, Switzerland, Thyssen-Bornemisza Collection,
no. 648

Formerly in the church at Jeziorak in Poland and later in
the Figdor Collection, Vienna, this is a complete and well
preserved vase carpet in an unusually small format. On the
red ground the main stems, in sky blue, yellow and ivory,
no longer have the sinuous curvilinear character of those
in the early vase carpet, no. 78, but have grown stiffer,
forming lattices of nearly hexagonal form. The arabesque
border and the geometrically patterned vases also suggest
a relatively late date, hardly earlier than the middle of the
17th century. Even though the design has lost its first
freshness and brilliance, the later vase carpets are very

79

decorative and beautifully executed. This example has an
additional interest through its provenance from an old
European church collection.

Literature
Beattie, 1972, no. 1.

80 Sickle-leaf rug

Persia, possibly Kerman, first half 17th century
L. 263 cm. W. 188 cm.
Washington, D.C., The Corcoran Gallery of Art,
no. 26–278; Bequest of William A. Clark, 1926
REPRODUCED IN COLOUR PAGE 46

This exquisite rug has the same technical characteristics as
the vase rugs and its field and border designs are closely
related to the earliest examples of that class. But the
swelling blossoms of the vase rugs are here reduced and
the energy of the design has been transferred into the pairs
of sickle-shaped leaves which form swirls of rotation and
counter-rotation along the length of the rug (an effect
which is still more marked in a large sickle-leaf carpet in
the Gulbenkian Foundation, Lisbon). The present design
lacks the severe internal logic of the vase design, with its
triple lattice of intersecting stems, and is a sophisticated
hybridization, including elements from other design
concepts. Here the main stems bearing the sickle-leaves
and large blossoms meander inconsequentially, intersecting
with a variety of trees and shrubs depicted on a much

smaller scale, as if a garden landscape were glimpsed through a tangle of briars. The quarter-flowers in two of the corners and the half medallions at the opposite end seem to hint at a medallion-and-corner design and it may be that this rug represents one half of the design for a longer carpet in which three complete medallions would have appeared at the centre. The asymmetry and the courtly elegance of the rug gave rise to Arthur Upham Pope's suggestion that it might have been made for a throne dais, whence the designation, the Corcoran throne rug, which is often bestowed on it. The rug is generally assigned to the first half of the 17th century, but earlier dates have sometimes been proposed. Rotatory or spinning motifs, as in this carpet, become prominent in European textile design about the middle of the 17th century.

Literature
Pope, 1939, p. 2384 ff., pl. 1234; Ellis, 1968, p. 19; Beattie, 1976, no. 15.

80

81 Carpet with vase design

India, Mughal empire, 17th century
L. 1596 cm. W. 325 cm.
John Hewett Collection
REPRODUCED IN COLOUR PAGE 48

Formerly in the Kevorkian Collection, this much-repaired Mughal carpet astonishes by its immense length of nearly 16 metres. It was obviously specially commissioned, presumably as a palace furnishing. The Emperor Jahangir (1605–28) has been suggested as a possible patron, but the style suggests that it is more likely to have been made in the period of Shah Jahan (1628–58) or Aurangzeb (1658–1707). The design is adapted from that of Persian

vase carpets, perhaps influenced by a variant type including lobed medallions (examples in museums in London, Sarajevo and Williamsburg). On the red ground great thorny stems in three different colours curve and intersect, forming three enormous curvilinear lattices; other thinner stems coil among these. All the stems carry blossoms in the style of Persian vase carpets and leaves in the shape of fish, which also occur in the Persian prototypes (cf. no. 80); there are also a few vases. At the main junctions of the lattices, down the centre and along the edges of the field, are various large medallions, some of them in shapes reminiscent of north-west Persian carpets. The sixteen-lobed central medallion is full of fish, like the pools and canals depicted in garden carpets; other medallions are in the form of eight-pointed stars, squares and pointed ovals. The border, with three guard stripes on either side, is designed on a much smaller scale than the field; it has a pattern of lobed cartouches containing arabesques and flowers, on a light blue background with cloud-bands. The design as a whole is an eclectic production, with elements derived from many different sources, and is notable for its scale and its variety rather than its elegance. The Mughal workshops seem to have made something of a speciality of immense carpets. They produced one even larger than this, about 18 metres by 9, to be installed at the very heart of the Persian empire, the Palace of the Forty Columns at Isfahan, where it was traditionally said to have arrived 'from distant lands on two elephants'; fragments of it are in the Victoria and Albert Museum, London and the University Museum, Philadelphia.

Literature
Sotheby's sale catalogue, London, 11th December 1970, lot 11.

81 (detail)

Flowering plant carpets

Patterns of more or less naturalistic flowering plants, either in offset rows against a plain background, or else in some form of lattice, were widely used in European textiles and embroideries from the late 16th century onwards. European patterns of this type seem to have had a great influence in Mughal India in the early 17th century, an influence which was no doubt strongly reinforced by the lively Mughal interest in gardens, in flowers and in botanical illustrations from Europe and elsewhere. During the reign of Shah Jahan (1628–58) designs of this kind were much favoured in Mughal textiles and carpets and it is interesting to see that fashion evidently decreed that even the forms of the lattice patterns should follow foreign, generally European, models (nos. 82–4). A little later, probably through the influence of the Mughal textiles and carpets, flowering plant designs also appeared in Persia (no. 86).

The flowering plant rugs show the very high quality of the designers, dyers and carpet weavers working for the Mughal court. But the most astonishing achievements of these craftsmen were the luxurious prayer rugs, which were no doubt specially commissioned, perhaps by the Emperor himself, and of which only two or three precious examples survive. They have flowering plant designs, executed in lustrous Kashmir wool, with knotting so fine that it surpasses almost all other carpets and rivals the most sumptuous velvets (no. 85).

Literature
Dimand, 1973, pp. 122–5.

82 Flowering plant rug

fragment

India, Mughal empire, second quarter or middle 17th century
L. 142 cm. W. 89 cm.
London, Victoria and Albert Museum, T.403–1910;
Salting Bequest

Formerly in the collection of George Salting, this fragment has a silk warp and weft and a finely knotted woollen pile, with about 90 knots per square centimetre. It is a good example of the high quality of carpet weaving and dyeing found in the small rugs made for the Mughal court. A smaller fragment probably from the same rug is in Düsseldorf. The design of naturalistic flowering plants within a curvilinear lattice was a popular one in the period of Shah Jahan. It has been suggested that the serrated bands of the lattice were inspired by similar curvilinear lattice patterns in Turkish silk textiles of the 17th century, many of which were imported for use at the Mughal court.

Literature
Kendrick & Tattersall, 1922, pl. 32; London, 1982, no. 200.

83 Flowering plant rug

fragments

India, Mughal empire, second quarter or middle
17th century
L. 94 cm. W. 79 cm.
The Keir Collection

This assemblage of fragments is a little confused but serves to give some idea of a fine Mughal rug of interesting design; a smaller assemblage of fragments from the same rug is in the Victoria and Albert Museum, London. The warp is of white cotton, the weft of red silk, and the pile of finely knotted wool, with about 80 knots per square centimetre. The layout of compartments in the shape of eight-pointed stars, with cross-shaped compartments between them, is an ancient one in Islamic art. But here it has been modernized by European

82

83

influences, which are apparent both in the naturalistic flowering plants and in the bar-and-leaf design of the compartment frames, reminiscent of European plasterwork. Similar stylistic elements recur in the ceiling decorations of the palace of Shah Jahan at Delhi.

Literature
Spuhler, 1978, no. 60; London, 1982, no. 201.

84 Flowering plant rug

fragments

India, Mughal empire, second quarter or middle
17th century
L. 121 cm. W. 137 cm.
City of Bristol Museum and Art Gallery, no. Or.1977.09.01;
Oriental Section

This is an assemblage of fragments from a carpet with a silk warp and weft and a finely knotted pile. On the crimson ground the green curvilinear lattice, with a complex bar-and-leaf design, shows European influence. Within the compartments of the lattice are symmetrical flowering plants of two different types, at right angles to each other, and inverted at each repetition. The scale and nature of the design suggest that this may have been a carpet of fairly large size, but no other fragments of it seem to be unknown.

Unpublished.

Formerly in the Aynard Collection, Lyon, and for this reason often called the Aynard prayer rug, this is an exquisite example of the finest designing, dyeing and weaving produced by the carpet workshops attached to the court of Shah Jahan. The warp and weft are of silk; the pile is of lustrous *pashm*, or Kashmir wool, dyed in more than fifteen shades; the knotting is so fine, with 174 knots per square centimetre, that it looks like a velvet rather than a knotted carpet.

On the red ground beneath the arch appears a large flowering plant, full of life and movement, with fantastic blossoms and twisting leaves, reminiscent of those seen in English embroidery. The little scudding clouds are a Chinese motif which was adopted in a number of Mughal textiles. From the earth at the bottom of the rug spring smaller flowering plants and on either side are cypress trees, a characteristic feature of many later Indian prayer rugs. The incomplete borders and the fact that the rug seems to have been repaired with patches from another similar piece have given rise to the suggestion that this may originally have been one panel of a multiple prayer rug rather than a separate rug.

Literature
Beattie, 1972, no. 9; London, 1982, no. 199.

84

85

85 Prayer rug

incomplete

India, Mughal empire, second quarter or middle
17th century
L. 124.5 cm. W. 90 cm.
Lugano, Switzerland, Thyssen-Bornemisza Collection,
no. 664a
REPRODUCED IN COLOUR PAGE 47

86

86 Flowering plant rug

fragment

Persia, possibly Kerman, middle or second half
17th century
L. 125 cm. W. 64 cm.
Washington, D.C., The Textile Museum, no. R33.3.2

This charming fragment is in the vase carpet technique
and is generally attributed to Kerman. The pattern of
offset rows of flowering plants was no doubt influenced by
Mughal carpets and textiles, in which this was a favourite
design, for example in an extensive group of mid
17th century carpets made at Lahore. The Indian designs
were inspired by European examples and it is interesting
to see European influence affecting Persian design by way
of Mughal India. In this fragment, the prettily drawn
plants, all different, are stylized into roughly oviform
shapes, but retain natural curves and traces of asymmetry,
unlike later Persian rugs of this type, where the plants are
much stiffer. The green background, instead of the more
usual red, helps to create a pleasing illusion of a flowering
meadow. The more formal border, showing two opposed
arabesques interlacing with a floral stem, is found on a
number of other types of carpets assigned to Kerman.
The inner guard stripe has a reciprocal 'heart' pattern,
the outer guard stripe a floral stem.

Literature
Ellis, 1968, p. 28; Beattie, 1976, no. 13.

On the making of carpets

May H. Beattie

This essay was written for the catalogue accompanying the exhibition,
Islamic Carpets from the Collection of Joseph V. McMullan,
which was presented by the Arts Council at the Hayward Gallery in 1972.
It is reprinted here with the kind consent of Dr Beattie.

It is now recognized that carpet weaving is a craft of far greater antiquity than was at one time supposed. Richly coloured, supple rugs with velvety pile were already being woven in the first millennium BC, and their structure is exactly the same as that found in modern carpets.

The remarkable persistence of the craft is not surprising as the carpet holds a unique place in the domestic life of the Orient. It is far more than a floor covering in the Occidental sense, for this single item may replace a great variety of articles such as tables, chairs, beds, coverlids, pictures, altar-cloths, cradles, stretchers, shrouds, and palls.

Origins

Originally sheep-rearing people who lacked sufficient furs for their needs, but who had wool available from their flocks, may have contrived the carpet as a substitute for an animal pelt. When patterns were introduced uniform clipping of the shaggy pile would follow in order to show up the designs more precisely. We do not know what types of looms were used for the weaving of the Bashadar fragment from about the end of the 6th century BC, or the almost complete Pazyryk carpet from over a century later, but obviously the craft is traditional and the technique and probably also types of equipment persist, as shown by a primitive warp-weighted loom which was seen in use in Meshed early this century.

Structure

The foundation of a carpet consists of warp and weft. The former extends from end to end of the carpet and eventually, when cut, forms the fringes. During weaving the warp yarn must be kept under even tension. This is a function of the loom. The weft which binds the warps together is passed from side to side as if threaded over and under alternate warps by means of a needle. In fact, this effect, as in cloth weaving, is achieved much more simply and quickly by so arranging the warps that alternate threads are separated into an upper and a lower plane. The weft is slipped through the resulting space, or 'shed', and is returned after the warps have been reversed by one or other of a variety of shedding devices. In kilims, which have no pile, the number of wefts per linear inch exceeds the number of warps. This results in a flat-woven weft-faced fabric resembling a European tapestry; and the yarn, instead of passing right across the rug, is returned as required to form the pattern. When a supplementary weft is used for the pattern it lies between the passes of foundation weft. The method of progression is usually to lead the yarn forward over two or four warps and back under one or two. Successive rows may be parallel or countered. This form of brocading is known as Soumak work. In the case of pile rugs the so-called knots lie between the foundation wefts. They are normally tied to every pair of warps, and when each row is completed the weft or wefts are passed. Side and end finishes vary. Sides may have a flat selvage or be overcast in various ways, all of which is done in the course of weaving. Yarn may be bi-coloured and tassels added. Ends vary from simple fringes to complex cross-weaving or ornate shell, or other supplementary, decoration. To produce a rich effect the ordinary cotton fringes are sometimes replaced by silk ones which are worked into the foundation of the rug.

Equipment

Looms vary in size from the modern but rarely seen miniature learner's loom, to the great looms of India, one of which had beams 48 feet wide and could take a carpet 100 feet in length. They may be modified in different ways but what determines local preference is not always evident.

The horizontal loom, which can either be pegged into the ground or stretched by means of side supports, is an obvious convenience for nomads as it can be dismantled easily, rolled up and packed onto an animal for transportation to the next site.

Vertical, or near vertical, looms have frames with either fixed or rotating beams. The Persian village loom consists of a simple rectangular framework at which the weaver works, and her bench is raised at intervals to a suitable height as the work proceeds. This loom is quite convenient provided that the length of the finished rug is less than the distance between the upper and lower beams. If it is longer, the warp has to be released and the woven part of the carpet brought down and reattached to the lower beam, sometimes by nailing. Even today rugs of extremely fine quality are woven on these simple frames, which makes one wonder if cottage weavers of several centuries ago, working at the instigation of merchants who provided materials more expensive than the weavers themselves could afford, were not responsible for some at least of the smaller so-called 'court' rugs.

The Tabriz loom, known in Turkey as the Bunyan or 'flat' loom, provides more scope because a rug almost twice the length of the distance between the beams can be woven. The warp is applied direct to the loom by two men who pass the yarn continuously up and down around the beams. Tension is controlled by wedges or jacks and when required the edge of the work can be pulled down to a level convenient to the weavers, the finished portion of the work being forced below the lower beam and up behind it. This is the type of loom preferred not only by the merchants of Tabriz, but also by those controlling modern commercial carpet weaving in Turkey.

The traditional village loom of Turkey is, however, the

roller-beam loom, which is also used in Kerman, in some other districts of Persia, in India, and further east. The warp is wound onto the upper beam and, as weaving proceeds, the finished part of the work is rolled, periodically, onto the lower beam while more yarn is unrolled from the upper one. Tension is controlled by a sturdy lever inserted into one of the holes in the warp beam and then lashed into place. The length of the carpet can be almost as long as the warp. In Turkey strings of cushion covers or rugs in series are woven on such looms, the parts being separated when they are cut down from the loom. Rugs may often be woven side by side on a loom of sufficient width. In Persia and India I have seen the weft yarn being passed right across all the rugs which, when the work was finished, were separated from each other by cutting. The raw edges were then firmly overcast, but the practice is obviously undesirable. In Turkey each rug on the loom was worked independently, the edges being properly finished as the work progressed.

The spindle is a tool of great antiquity, used alike by men and women. The wheel also has been known in the Orient for many centuries. Both are still used by spinsters for preparing rug yarn, if it is not bought ready-spun direct from a factory, and one can see women turning their little wheels in the household courtyards or twirling their spindles as they walk to market or sit in the doorways in the cool of the evening. Much of the yarn in antique Egyptian rugs has a twist which is opposite in direction to that found in most other types, possibly because of a different method of using the spindle.

Small pieces of equipment such as yarn-winders, comb-beaters used to press or beat the wefts into place, and rug-stretchers for maintaining an even width of rug during weaving, do not vary greatly, but in Tabriz additional equipment is used. A flat hook with a blade on one side is customary for knotting and cutting the yarn, and a long flat needle, like a pliable steel ruler, is used to pass the weft. When trimming is done on the loom the scissors may be simple or gauged according to the length of pile required, but large shears are usual if the trimming is to be done after removal of the carpet from the loom.

Materials

In the case of luxurious 'court' carpets materials of the finest quality are obviously needed and would be obtained whether they were available locally or not. The foundation of such rugs was often of silk, because the strength of the fibres in relation to their diameter makes it suitable for the weaving of fine carpets. In more ordinary rugs the materials would depend on what was available locally and on the economic conditions prevailing at the time. One expects woollen foundations in the rugs of pastoral people but cotton will be used if it is readily available and cheaper than wool. This is seen where, in recent years, cotton has been introduced into rug weaving areas and now replaces wool in the foundations of local rugs. The same types of yarn used in antique carpets continue to be used today. Wool is by far the most satisfactory pile yarn as it is resilient and takes dyes well. Quality is of first importance. The wool of Persia is renowned for its lustre and even an Anatolian carpet weaver will occasionally admit, somewhat grudgingly, that it is superior to that of Turkey. The fine undercoat of the Tibetan goat, which was used in Kashmir shawls, makes a remarkably beautiful pile. Other fibres such as silk, cotton (plain or mercerized), ramie, coarse hairs, and rayon have all been used in carpets to a greater or less extent.

Dyeing

Where weaving is largely a domestic craft, as in Anatolia, the yarn used in older rugs would, for the most part, be dyed on the premises and much time and trouble would go to the collection of materials and preparation of the dyes. A portable 'filing cabinet' was sometimes used. It took the form of a coat or jacket with many pockets into which the various plants and other raw materials were consigned as they were collected. These garments were scarce enough early this century, and now, no doubt, any that survive have been put to other uses following the introduction of more easily obtainable synthetic dyes. In Persia, according to 19th century writers, dyeing was usually the prerogative of the village dyer and the traditions were handed down from generation to generation as cherished secrets in families often of Jewish stock. An organic chemist could explain in simple terms the chemical reactions involved in dyeing but besides the obvious reactions the quality of the wool and water and the intensity of the sunlight seem to have contributed in less obvious ways to the beauty of colour in antique rugs, and the understanding and control of such factors was the point at which the craft of the dyer became an art. The effect of substances used in dyeing in some districts causes brittleness of the yarn fibres, notably when dark brown, red, and a certain green are used. The yarn so dyed wears away more quickly than that dyed with other colours and leaves part of the design standing out in relief.

The greatest disaster which ever befell the Oriental rug was Sir William Perkin's synthesis of mauveine in 1856. This revolutionized the dyeing industry in both West and East. No one can blame a village woman for going to the bazaar for synthetic dyes which are easy to get, easy to use and inexpensive. The range of shades in the new dyes was greater, the colours more brilliant, the results more uniform, and it was of little consequence to the weaver that some of the dyes were also fugitive. One only has to look at the faded repairs in museum carpets acquired in this unfortunate period – about thirty years on either side of 1900 – to realize the damage which these dyes did. Although present day dyes are largely synthetic, so far they are fairly stable. Contrary to popular belief the dyes in antique rugs often fade but the resulting colours may be more attractive than those which result from the fading of synthetic dyes.

Designs

Besides equipment and materials, designs are needed. The weaver may use a simple motif learned in childhood at her mother's side, but the charm of the rug she weaves depends on her choice of motif and her skill in the use of colours; or she may copy a design from the back of an existing rug where the pattern is more obvious than on the front. While such methods no doubt explain the amazing persistence of certain designs over a century or two, this constant repetition does seem to be a characteristic of weavers of Turkish stock. Through inherent inventiveness a weaver may create a simple new design, or she may counterpose or modify familiar motifs to avert the boredom of endless repetition, and, if left to her own devices, the designs will be single plane repeats. Among villagers such methods are to be expected as designing is costly and weavers are poor. In the case of great carpets of high quality, however, the designs must have been drawn in the fashionable style of the moment by experts and transferred to paper, the full size of the carpet if necessary, by copyists. Analysis of highly complex designs show that they must have been built up from a series of simple, curvilinear patterns, which were superimposed, one upon the other, with such skill that the balance of the finished design was unimpaired. In more modest symmetrical designs a cartoon of only a quarter of the design need be prepared. When coloured it is cut into sections, pasted onto cardboard and varnished to protect it from wear and tear. Considerable numbers of such cartoons can still be seen in some of the premises of long-established merchants. In Ushak the women are justly proud of their ability to weave a carpet from a small free-hand design without it being enlarged onto squared-paper. Villagers in the Heriz district of Persia have a similar skill but their designs when woven are rectilinear although that of the model may be curvilinear. Apart from cartoons a small woven sample, known in Turkey as a 'nümüne' and in Persia as 'wagireh' may be supplied to a weaver by the merchant for whom she works. This is still done but those used last century are now becoming collectors' treasures.

Surviving rugs provide a faint echo of great designs of the past, but many must be lost entirely, and one regrets that more travellers (unlike the one who mentioned the animal rugs of Kerman) did not leave even a brief description of the rugs they extolled in such glowing terms.

Warps and Wefts

Warps must be firmly spun and plied to give sufficient strength to bear the weight of the finished rug, whereas the weft yarn of pile rugs is loosely spun and often unplied, which makes it suitable for packing down on the knots to hold them in place. Very fine rugs are woven on silk foundations and in some Indian rugs the warps are arranged in stripes of different colours but not necessarily of the same width, as the purpose seems to have been to aid the weaver in executing a complicated design in a rug of fine quality. Even today in commercial rugs it is quite usual to see a dyed warp thread at intervals to keep the weaver on the right line, or a line drawn across the warps as a guide to keeping the rows straight. In certain antique Indian rugs the unevenness of the edge of the work was so marked that additional short lengths of weft had to be introduced in the course of weaving to correct the irregularities.

As foundation yarns are not obvious on the surface of a rug they provide an opportunity for using up dark yarn which is unsuitable for dyeing. In many cases, however, the weft yarn is dyed to harmonize with the field. In dragon rugs of the Caucasus, and kindred pieces, a thick cabled weft can often be seen at irregular intervals on the back of the rug and seems to be a 'stint' mark indicating how much work has been done in a given time, whereas in east Persian rugs a piece of yarn looped into the work and left hanging at the back an inch or so from the edge seems to serve a similar purpose. In provincial rugs the number of passes of weft varies and the more there are the longer will be the pile, the flatter will it lie and the less durable will the rug be. To avoid moving every time the weft is passed a weaver, especially if she works alone, will return the weft at a point within easy reach of where she sits, reducing the number of warps taken in in each row. After several inches of weaving are completed the adjoining section is worked. This results in diagonal lines, visible on the back of the rug, where the wefts meet. These lines are seen most often in certain Ottoman and Indian rugs.

One difference between antique rugs and those from the 'revival' period in the 19th century is that many of the great antique rugs are woven with three passes of weft after each row of knots, whereas in late rugs two passes are much more usual. Just when this, and the greater use of the symmetrical Turkish knot in rugs of north-west Persia, began, is not known.

Knots

A good Oriental weaver can tie at least 10,000 knots in an eight-hour day, which is about four times the speed of some of the carpet weavers of western Europe. Counts vary from four or five to the square inch to over 2,000. A rug with a high knot count should wear much better than one which is coarsely woven, but this does not mean that it is aesthetically more desirable. The richness of colour and the charm of good traditional abstract designs in coarsely woven Anatolian and Caucasian rugs, often not older than the 19th century, have far greater appeal for many people, particularly in the West, than the beautifully woven but rather anaemic looking rugs with a high knot count which became fashionable last century and are still woven in great numbers. Today, and probably in the past, rugs of exceptional quality are woven only to order, but four or five lower grades are produced for ordinary trade purposes. Various types of knots are, or have been, used in different parts of the rug-weaving world, and unusual methods of tying are still practised by Spanish, Berber, and Tibetan weavers; and from time to time one also finds curiously tied knots in rugs where those of more usual type would be expected. It has been customary to refer to the two most commonly used knots by proper names which are both irrelevant and misleading and it is high time that they were replaced by descriptive rather than geographical terms.

Where exactly the knots were first used will never be known but the so-called Persian or Senna knot was the one used by the weavers of the Bashadar fragment. The terms 'asymmetrical' or 'open' knot could be used to describe this type and they have no geographical implications. The yarn is passed between two adjoining warps, looped round one, passed back over it and under the second warp so that the ends of yarn lie on either side of, and are kept open by, the second warp. It is usually tied with the ends coming up on either side of the left warp thread (open-on-the-left) but the form open-on-the-right is also used.

The so-called Turkish or Ghiordes knot may equally well be described as the 'symmetrical' or 'closed' knot. This was the one used by the weavers of the Pazyryk carpet. The yarn is passed between two warps, looped under one, passed back over both and brought to the surface again between the two warps, so that the two ends of the pile yarn lie together enclosed by the collar of the knot.

The open knot is usual in finely woven carpets in curvilinear designs, the closed knot more often in robust, richly coloured village rugs. To generalize briefly and broadly, for there are many exceptions in these matters, the asymmetrical knot open-on-the-left is found in Egyptian rugs, in Turkish 'court' rugs, in most of the great antique rugs of Persia, and in those of India, in many of the somewhat later rugs of Persia, western and eastern Turkestan, and China, and in the commercially produced late rugs of Turkey. The asymmetrical knot open-on-the-right is quite usual in Turkman rugs as well as that open-on-the-left.

The symmetrical or closed knot is preferred by weavers of

Asymmetrical or open knot
(Persian or Senna)
open-on-the-left

Asymmetrical or open knot
(Persian or Senna)
open-on-the-right

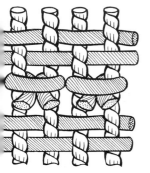

mmetrical or closed knot
urkish or Ghiordes)

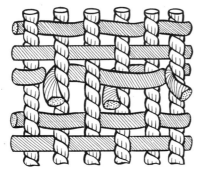

Paired or jufti or false knot
an asymmetrical or open form

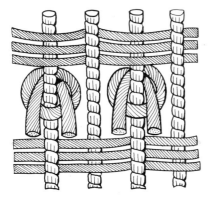

Spanish knot

traditional Turkish village rugs, by those of the Caucasus, by many of the villagers of western Persia (including those of Senna), and by some Turkman weavers, particularly Yomuds, of north-eastern Persia and the U.S.S.R.

The open and closed knots are sometimes found in one rug, used quite indiscriminately, and, in certain Turkman rugs, and in those from further east, the rows may be neatly finished at one or both ends with the closed knot, although the rest of the rug is woven in an open knot.

Another knot found in many antique rugs is the jufti (paired) or false knot, which in asymmetrical form is tied in various ways over two pairs of warps. The symmetrical form is relatively rare. It is unfortunate that the use of this knot is increasing as rugs so woven lack sufficient pile yarn and in consequence wear poorly.

It is customary to weave pile carpets with the knots on one side only but fragments of antique rugs exist which show that a built-in underlay was achieved by tying knots also on the back of the rug. This was done at intervals of several rows of the surface knots and the yarn was left long and so formed an admirable pad as additional protection against the cold of the floor. The practice is continued, particularly in Anatolia, where such pieces are known as 'two-faced' rugs. Some are extremely finely woven with different designs on the two surfaces and are examples of technical virtuosity rather than rugs for practical purposes.

Weavers

When all the equipment, materials and designs are assembled the weavers begin their time-consuming work. For centuries Oriental carpets have been mentioned in documents but the references are brief and concern provenance rather than weavers or methods of weaving. Both the Mughal Emperor Akbar and Shah Abbas of Persia established carpet workshops, and some at least of the glittering silk and gold rugs came from looms in the royal precincts just off the great maidan in Isfahan. We are not told how these carpets were woven but no doubt the methods were analogous to those used by Persian weavers who settled in eastern India in the 16th century. In 1679 their descendants were still working in Ellore. The looms they used were vertical, the warps were cotton, a master weaver who directed the boy-weavers, 'called' the pattern from a paper cartoon, and the rough ends of the knots were trimmed with scissors. The description could apply to carpet weaving in many places today. At this time also boys were employed in carpet weaving in Egypt and China. Indeed when the Emperor visited Ning Hsia in 1697 he was not only presented with carpets but was sufficiently interested to order the weavers to demonstrate how the work was done. Unfortunately the details were not recorded, but the 'foot carpets' presented to the Emperor were described as being coarser than those of Turkey, as indeed many Chinese rugs are.

In the few early descriptions women are not mentioned as carpet weavers, although among nomads and in Anatolia in particular carpet weaving is largely woman's work; but in a Muslim country three hundred years ago one would hardly expect a foreigner of the opposite sex to have access to the premises where women were working. Apart from domestic weaving the further East one goes the more does carpet weaving seem to become the prerogative of men.

This splendid exhibition provides an opportunity to compare and contrast not only colour and design but also some of the less obvious yet important features of carpets, such as qualities and types of yarns, regional colour ranges and characteristics of side and end finishes, all of which combine to produce the rich and overwhelming beauty of the Oriental carpet.

Bibliography

Atil, E., *Renaissance of Islam: Art of the Mamluks*, 1981.

Batári, F., *Alte Anatolische Teppiche aus dem Museum für Kunstgewerbe in Budapest*, 1974; catalogue of an exhibition at the Steiermärkisches Landesmuseum Joanneum, Graz.
Batári, F., *Frühosmanische Knüpfteppiche*, 1982; catalogue of an exhibition at the Dobo Varmuzeum, Eger.
Beattie, M. H., 'Antique Rugs at Hardwick Hall', *Oriental Art*, v, no. 2, 1959, pp. 3–12.
Beattie, M., *The Rug in Islamic Art*, 1964; catalogue of an exhibition at Temple Newsam House, Leeds.
Beattie, M., 'Britain and the Oriental Carpet', *Leeds Art Calendar*, no. 55, 1964, pp. 4–15.
Beattie, M. H., 'Coupled-column Prayer Rugs', *Oriental Art*, XIV, 1968, pp. 243–58.
Beattie, M. H., *The Thyssen-Bornemisza Collection of Oriental Rugs*, 1972.
Beattie, M. H., *Carpets of Central Persia*, 1976; catalogue of an exhibition at the Mappin Art Gallery, Sheffield, and the City Museum and Art Gallery, Birmingham.
Beattie, M., Housego, J., and Morton, A. H., 'Vase-technique Carpets and Kirman', *Oriental Art*, XXIII, 1977, pp. 455–71.
Bennett, I. (editor), *Rugs and Carpets of the World*, 1977.
Berlin, Museum für Islamische Kunst, *Katalog*, 1979.
Bernheimer, O., *Alte Teppiche des 16. bis 18. Jahrhunderts der Firma L. Bernheimer*, 1959.
Bode, W. von, and Kühnel, E., *Vorderasiatische Knüpfteppiche aus alter Zeit*, 1955.
Boralevi, A., 'The Discovery of two Great Carpets: The Cairene Carpets of the Medici,' *Hali*, v, no. 3, 1983.

Cammann, S., 'Symbolic Meanings in Oriental Rug Patterns', *Textile Museum Journal*, III, no. 3, 1974.
Cammann, S., 'Cosmic Symbolism on Carpets from the Sanguszko Group', *Studies in Art and Literature of the Near East*, edited by Peter Chelkowski, 1974.
Cammann, S., 'The Systematic Study of Oriental Rugs: Techniques and Patterns', *Journal of the American Oriental Society*, vol. 95, 1975, pp. 248–60.
Cavallo, A. S., 'A Carpet from Cairo', *Journal of the American Research Center in Egypt*, I, 1962, pp. 69–74.
Cox, R., *L'Art de Décorer les Tissus*, 1900.

Denny, W. B., 'Ten Great Carpets, Boston Museum of Fine Arts, Autumn 1977', *Hali*, I, no. 2, 1978, pp. 156–64.
Denny, W. B., 'The Origin of the Designs of Ottoman Court Carpets', *Hali*, II, no. 1, 1979, pp. 6–11.
Denny, W. B., 'Türkmen Rugs and Early Rug Weaving in the Western Islamic World,' *Hali*, IV, no. 4, 1982, pp. 329–37.
Dimand, M. S., *The Ballard Collection of Oriental Rugs in the City Art Museum of St. Louis*, 1935.
Dimand, M. S., and Mailey, J., *Oriental Rugs in The Metropolitan Museum of Art*, 1973.
Durul, Y., and Aslanapa, O., *Selçuklu Halilari*, n.d.

Ellis, C. G., 'Gifts from Kashan to Cairo', *Textile Museum Journal*, I, no. 1, 1962, pp. 33–46.
Ellis, C. G., 'A Soumak-Woven Rug in a 15th century International Style', *Textile Museum Journal*, I, no. 2, 1963, pp. 3–20.
Ellis, C. G., 'Some Compartment Designs for Carpets, and Herat', *Textile Museum Journal*, I, no. 4, 1965, pp. 42–56.
Ellis, C. G., 'Mysteries of the Misplaced Mamluks', *Textile Museum Journal*, II, no. 2, 1967, pp. 2–20.
Ellis, C. G., 'Kirman's Heritage in Washington: Vase Rugs in the Textile Museum', *Textile Museum Journal*, II, no. 3, 1968, pp. 17–34.
Ellis, C. G., 'The Ottoman Prayer Rugs', *Textile Museum Journal*, II, no. 4, 1969, pp. 5–22.
Ellis, C. G., 'The "Lotto" Pattern as a Fashion in Carpets', *Festschrift für Peter Wilhelm Meister*, 1975, pp. 19–31.
Ellis, C. G., 'The Portuguese Carpets of Gujarat', *Islamic Art in The Metropolitan Museum of Art*, edited by Richard Ettinghausen, 1975.
Enderlein, V., 'Zwei Agyptische Gebetsteppiche im Islamischen Museum', *Forschungen und Berichte, Staatliche Museen zu Berlin*, XIII, 1971, pp. 7–15.
Erdmann, K., *Orientalische Teppiche aus vier Jahrhunderten*, 1950; catalogue of an exhibition at the Museum für Kunst und Gewerbe, Hamburg.
Erdmann, K., *Der Orientalische Knüpfteppich*, 1955.
Erdmann, K., 'Zu einem Anatolischen Teppichfragment aus Fostat', *Istanbuler Mitteilungen*, 6, 1955, pp. 41–51.
Erdmann, K., 'Neuere Untersuchungen zur Frage der Kairener Teppiche', *Ars Orientalis*, IV, 1961, pp. 65–105.
Erdmann, K., *Europa und der Orientteppich*, 1962.
Erdmann, K., 'Weniger Bekannte Ushak-Muster', *Kunst des Orients*, 4, 1963, pp. 79–97.
Erdmann, K., *Seven Hundred Years of Oriental Carpets*, 1970.
Erdmann, K., *The History of the Early Turkish Carpet*, 1977.
Ettinghausen, R., 'New Light on Early Animal Carpets', *Aus der Welt des Islam, Festschrift für Ernst Kühnel*, 1959, pp. 93–116.
Ettinghausen, R., *Persian Art, Calouste Gulbenkian Collection*, 1972.
Ettinghausen, R., Dimand, M. S., Mackie, L. M. and Ellis, C. G., *Prayer Rugs*, 1974; catalogue of an exhibition at the Textile Museum, Washington D.C.

Ferrandis Torres, J., *Exposición de Alfombras Antiguas Españolas*, 1933.

Irwin, J., *The Girdlers' Carpet*, 1962.

Kendrick, A. F., *Victoria and Albert Museum, Guide to the Collection of Carpets*, 1915.
Kendrick, A. F., and Tattersall, C. E. C., *Hand-Woven Carpets: Oriental and European*, 1922.
King, D., Pinner, R., and Franses, M., 'East Mediterranean Carpets in the Victoria & Albert Museum', *Hali*, IV, no. 1, 1981, pp. 36–52.
Kühnel, E., and Bellinger, L., *The Textile Museum, Catalogue of Spanish Rugs, 12th Century to 19th Century*, 1953.
Kühnel, E., and Bellinger, L., *Cairene Rugs and Others Technically Related*, 1957.

Lamm, C. J., 'The Marby Rug and some Fragments of Carpets found in Egypt', *Orientaliska Sällskapets Årsbok*, 1937, pp. 51–130.
London, Victoria and Albert Museum, *The Indian Heritage: Court Life and Arts under Mughal Rule*; exhibition catalogue, 1982.

Mackie, L., *The Splendour of Turkish Weaving*, 1973; catalogue of an exhibition at the Textile Museum, Washington D.C.
Mackie, L. W., 'A Turkish Carpet with Spots and Stripes', *Textile Museum Journal*, IV, no. 3, 1976, pp. 5–20.
Mackie, L., 'Two Remarkable Fifteenth Century Carpets from Spain', *Textile Museum Journal*, IV, no. 4, 1977, pp. 15–32.
Mackie, L., 'Native and Foreign Influences in Carpets woven in Spain during the 15th century', *Hali*, II, no. 2, 1979, pp. 88–95.
Mańkowski, T., 'Note on the Cost of Kashan Carpets at the Beginning of the Seventeenth Century', *Bulletin of the American Institute for Persian Art and Archaeology*, New York, VI, 1936, p. 152 ff.
Mańkowski, T., *Polskie Tkaniny i Hafty XVI–XVIII Wieku*, 1954.
Martin, F. R., *A. History of Oriental Carpets before 1800*, 1908.
May, F. L., 'Hispano-Moresque Rugs', *Notes Hispanic*, The Hispanic Society of America, V, 1945, pp. 30–69.
Mills, J., 'Early Animal Carpets in Western Paintings – A Review,' *Hali*, I, no. 3, 1978, pp. 234–43.
Mills, J., 'Small Pattern Holbein Carpets in Western Paintings', *Hali*, I, no. 4, 1978, pp. 326–34.
Mills, J., 'East Mediterranean Carpets in Western Paintings', *Hali*, IV, no. 1, 1981, pp. 53–5.
Mills, J., '"Lotto" Carpets in Western Paintings,' *Hali*, III, no. 4, 1981, pp. 278–89.
Mumford, J. K., *The Yerkes Collection of Oriental Carpets*, 1910.

Öz, T., *Turkish Ceramics*, n.d.

Pinner, R., and Stanger, J., 'Kufic Borders on Small Pattern Holbein Carpets', *Hali*, I, no. 4, 1978, pp. 335–8.
Pope, A. U., *Catalogue of a Loan Exhibition of Early Oriental Carpets*, The Art Club of Chicago, 1926.
Pope, A. U., *A Survey of Persian Art*, 1939.

Sarre, F., 'A Fourteenth Century Spanish "Synagogue" Carpet', *Burlington Magazine*, LVI, 1930, pp. 89–95.
Sarre, F., and Trenkwald, H., *Old Oriental Carpets*, I, 1926, II, 1929.
Spuhler, F., 'Der Figurale Kaschan-Wirkteppich aus den Sammlungen des Regierenden Fürsten von Liechtenstein', *Kunst des Orients*, V, 1968, pp. 55–61.
Spuhler, F., *Islamic Carpets and Textiles in the Keir Collection*, 1978.

Tattersall, C. E. C., *A History of British Carpets*, 1934.

Unger, E. de, 'An Ancestor of the Mamluk Carpets', *Hali*, V, no. 1, 1982, pp. 44–6.

Van de Put, A., 'Some Fifteenth-Century Spanish Carpets', *Burlington Magazine*, XIX, 1911, pp. 344–50.
Van de Put, A., 'A Fifteenth-Century Spanish Carpet', *Burlington Magazine*, XLV, 1924, pp. 119–20.
Végh, G., and Layer, K., edited by Dall'Oglio, M. and C., *Turkish Rugs in Transylvania*, 1977.
Völker, A., 'Überlegungen zur Neuaufstellung der Orientteppichsammlung des Österreichischen Museums für angewandte Kunst in Wien', *Hali*, II, no. 1, 1979, pp. 12–15.

Whiting, M., 'The Red Dyes of some East Mediterranean Carpets', *Hali*, IV, no. 1, 1981, pp. 55–6.

Yetkin, S., *Türk Hali Sanati*, 1974.

Zick, J., 'Eine Gruppe von Gebetsteppichen und ihre Datierung', *Berliner Museen, Berichte aus den ehem. Preuss. Kunstsammlung*, Neue Folge, Jg. II, 1961, pp. 6–14.

Photographic credits

The publishers wish to thank the owners of works reproduced in this catalogue
for kindly granting permissions and for providing photographs.
Photographs have been supplied by owners and by those listed below.

BLACK AND WHITE

Ed. Alinari, Venice: front endpaper
A. C. Cooper Ltd.: fig. 16
L. Bernheimer K.G.: no. 12
Marcello Bertoni, Florence: nos. 21, 56
By courtesy of Eskenazi Ltd., Milan: back endpaper
John Mills Photography, Ltd., Liverpool: fig. 14
Narbutt-Lieven, Vienna: nos. 22, 30, 74
Service Photographique de la Réunion des musées nationaux,
    Paris: figs. 18, 22
Studio Granath, Stockholm: no. 65
L. Sully-Jaulmes: nos. 46, 50
Eileen Tweedy: nos. 81, 83
Courtesy of Victoria and Albert Museum, London: figs. 35, 38,
    nos. 32, 33, 37, 70, 76
Mike Williams: no. 36

COLOUR

Marcello Bertoni, Florence: nos. 21, 56
Karl-Erik Granath: no. 65
Eileen Tweedy: no. 81